TYNESIDE NEIGHBOURHOODS

Tyneside Neighbourhoods

Deprivation, Social Life and
Social Behaviour in One British City

Daniel Nettle

OpenBook
Publishers

http://www.openbookpublishers.com

© 2015 Daniel Nettle

All external links were active on 2 December 2015 and have been archived via the Internet Archive Wayback Machine at https://archive.org/web

Open Data: The extensive dataset compiled by the author as part of the research project reported in this publication is freely available at https://osf.io/ys7g6

An archived version of the dataset, preserving the data in the form it was at the time of publication, is available at http://dx.doi.org/10.17605/OSF.IO/W9Z2P

Updated digital material and resources associated with this volume are available at http://www.openbookpublishers.com/isbn/9781783741885#resources

ISBN Paperback: 978-1-78374-188-5
ISBN Hardback: 978-1-78374-189-2
ISBN Digital (PDF): 978-1-78374-190-8
ISBN Digital ebook (epub): 978-1-78374-191-5
ISBN Digital ebook (mobi): 978-1-78374-192-2
DOI: 10.11647/OBP.0084

Cover image: Back lane, Newcastle upon Tyne. Photo by Daniel Nettle (CC BY 4.0).

All paper used by Open Book Publishers is SFI (Sustainable Forestry Initiative), PEFC (Programme for the Endorsement of Forest Certification Schemes) and Forest Stewardship Council(r)(FSC(r) certified.

Printed in the United Kingdom, United States and Australia
by Lightning Source for Open Book Publishers (Cambridge, UK).

Contents

It's oh, but, aa ken well, ah, you me hinny burd,
The bonny lass of Benwell, ah, you, ah.
She's lang-legged and mother-like, ah, you hinny burd
See her raking up the dyke, ah, you, ah.

The Quayside for sailors, ah, you me hinny burd,
The Castle Garth for tailors, ah, you, ah.
The Gateshead Hills for millers, ah, you hinny burd,
The North Shore for keelers, ah, you, ah.

There's Sandgate for owld rags, ah, you, me hinny burd,
And Gallowgate for trolley bags; ah, you, ah.
There's Denton and Kenton, ah you, hinny burd,
And canny Langbenton, ah, you, ah.

There's Tynemouth and Cullercoats, ah, you me hinny burd,
And North Shields for sculler boats; ah, you, ah.
There's Westoe lies in a neuk, ah, you hinny burd,
And South Shields the place for seut, ah, you, ah.

There's Horton and Hollywell, ah, you me hinny burd
And bonny Seaton Delaval; ah, you ah.
Hartley Pans for sailors, ah, you hinny burd
And Bedlington for nailers, ah, you ah.

Traditional Tyneside song

1. Introduction

It's like a jungle sometimes. It makes me wonder,
How I keep from going under.[1]

Prelude

This book is a study of people's social relationships and social behaviour in different neighbourhoods of one English conurbation, Tyneside. I define social behaviour in the classic biological sense, to mean things that one individual does that have consequences for another individual or individuals (Bourke, 2011; Hamilton, 1964). Thus, merely being present at the same place as another individual is not necessarily a social behaviour. Giving something to them, taking something from them, improving their environment or despoiling it are all social behaviours. Social behaviours can be further classified as prosocial, where the actor's actions improve someone else's situation, or antisocial, where they make it worse. For the most part, the book is based on comparative data from two particular neighbourhoods within the city of Newcastle upon Tyne, which I will call A and B. There is also some ancillary data from other parts of Tyneside. The book is based on several years of intermittent fieldwork by several people; I will say more about this later in the chapter. First it is worth saying something about how the long journey that has led to this book got started.

In around 2007 or 2008, I had a chance conversation with my partner on the subject of household refuse. I lived in the North East of the city of

---

1   The epigraphs to all of the chapters in this book are from 'The Message', by Grandmaster Flash and the Furious Five, written by Joel Edwards, Robin Barter and Robert Post (1983).

                    http://dx.doi.org/10.11647/OBP.0084.01

Newcastle upon Tyne, whereas she lived in the West End, in the house we now live in together. Newcastle, like many cities, asks its citizens to divide household waste into recyclable and non-recyclable categories, collected on different days. I was uncertain, as I recall, about the proper categorization of some kind of plastic. I wanted to behave well and sort correctly, and was therefore anxious to have the right information about what the rules were. She said something to the effect that she wouldn't expend too much effort on getting things like this right, since her bin would be quite likely to be set fire to anyway before it could be collected.

It turned out that her attitude was not without foundation. Various things did indeed get set ablaze in that part of Newcastle at that time, a problem that thankfully seems to have abated somewhat. Even when recycling bins did not burn, they would often be either kicked over or used improperly by someone else once on the street, resulting in a mixed load that the recycling lorry would refuse to take. Thus, she was absolutely correct in her assessment of the futility of expending much effort in the direction of conscientious recycling; such effort would end up being undermined by the action of others. Her lightly-made comment made a remarkable impression on me, for several reasons.

First, over the years I have thought a fair amount about the age-old question of whether people are basically good (helpful, prosocial, cooperative), or whether they are basically selfish. This question has a very clear answer: it depends. Humans have motivations to deliver social benefits to others, but these are not their only motivations, and the expression of these motivations is contingent and conditional. Most obviously, and as illustrated by the blazing bin example, the expression of prosocial motivations depends on expectations about what others in the population might (or might not) do. This means that if you want to understand when people will behave prosocially and when they will not, you need to know a lot about their ecology (what kinds of things are going on in the surrounding population?), and you also need to know a lot about human psychology (how exactly do the information-processing mechanisms that take cues from the local environment in order to adjust an individual's social decisions work?).

The second reason that her comment struck me was that our respective houses were in the same city and only around 3km apart, yet clearly the behaviour going on around them was utterly different. Rubbish bins would never be set fire to where I lived. It was—and I mean this as more than a casual simile—like living in two different countries. Yet our two neighbourhoods shared the same language, ethnic heritage, national and local government, and judicial systems. In fact, the same council vehicles collected the refuse from the two places. This relates to the whole issue of the nature and scale of variation in human social behaviour, and in human culture more broadly. As social scientists, what should be our units of analysis: countries, cities, streets or individuals? How meaningful is it to talk about an English culture, when two samples of English people—two samples taken a 15-minute bicycle ride apart—give such different pictures?

Third, my partner had clearly and without much thought calibrated her actions to her ecology. She had a similar long-term developmental history to mine, and her fundamental social attitudes were the same as my own. Yet her neighbourhood environment had clearly caused her decision-making to change. Anthropologists call the process by which an individual's social behaviour is shaped by the surrounding population acculturation. However, many descriptions of acculturation envisage a slow, perhaps linguistically-mediated process lasting many years, typically happening to children as they grow into adults. My partner had moved to the neighbourhood already adult; what had happened to her seemed more like an immediate cognitive response to a certain kind of perceptual experience. This raises interesting questions about which experiences are important in acculturation, and the timescale over which they act. If I moved to the land where bins go up in flames, would my behaviour change? If so, which perceptual inputs would be most important in causing the change, and how quickly would it occur if I had them? And if the change occurred quickly, how quickly could it be reversed?

If one tributary stream of this book was a longstanding interest in prosocial and antisocial behaviour, the second tributary was an interest in socioeconomic deprivation and its consequences. I haven't told you, though it may not surprise you to learn, that the neighbourhood where recycling was overshadowed by arson was one where most people were extremely poor, whereas the orderly neighbourhood was one where most people were affluent. If there were large differences between our respective neighbourhoods in terms of prosocial and antisocial behaviour, we might be dealing with another instance of the near-ubiquitous phenomenon of the *social gradient*.

Social gradient is the term used by social scientists to describe any situation where the outcome we are interested in is patterned according to socioeconomic position, so that more affluent or high-status social groups look different from less affluent or lower-status ones. I may be coloured by the particular topics I have conducted research on, but social gradients strike me as the overwhelmingly salient fact about contemporary developed societies. If a Martian researcher asked me for a quick summary of how these societies work, I would give the following one: things work out differently for the rich and the poor. Social gradients have been described for many variables in the UK: birth weight, age at parenthood, paternal behaviour, breastfeeding, smoking, body mass, depression, and orientation towards the future, to name but a few (Adams & White, 2009; Nettle, 2008, 2010a; Pill, Peters, & Robling, 1995; Stansfeld & Head, 1998). Perhaps the most fundamental social gradient is that of life itself: the poor in the UK can expect to be alive several fewer years than the rich, and they can expect to be healthy for many fewer years (Adler, Boyce, & Chesney, 1994; Bajekal, 2005). Whether the gradient in the length of life is the cause or the consequence of all the other gradients is a delicate question. In my work, I have argued that there are often bidirectional relationships: poor people worry less about the long-term health consequences of smoking because they don't think they will remain alive so long anyway, regardless of what they do, but this in turn exacerbates the already-existing gap in how long they will live (Nettle, 2010b; Pepper & Nettle, 2014).

Social gradients connect in a number of ways to the issues about prosocial and antisocial behaviour that I have already discussed. Some of the social gradients that have been documented directly concern prosocial and antisocial behaviour: there are social gradients in crime, in violence, and in pro-environmental attitudes, for example (Dietz, Stern, & Guagnano, 1998; Kikuchi & Desmond, 2015; Sampson, Raudenbush, & Earls, 1997; Shaw, Tunstall, & Dorling, 2005). Moreover, social gradients lead us once again to the question of the scale of variation in human culture. Because of social gradients, the variation *within* contemporary societies is often more striking than the variation between them. For example, Figure 1.1 plots women's average age at first pregnancy for a number of countries, and then for two different groups of English women of White British ancestry: those who live in the most affluent decile of English neighbourhoods, and those who live in the most deprived decile. As you can see, the English women from the affluent neighbourhoods look like the average women from Switzerland or New Zealand. The English women from the deprived neighbourhoods behave like the average women of Guatemala or Kazakhstan. These groups of women often live just hundreds of metres apart, and yet we see that their lives are organized as differently from one another as Swiss women's are from Kazakh women. This is immediately reminiscent of my short journey across Newcastle from the land of recycling to the land of burning bins.

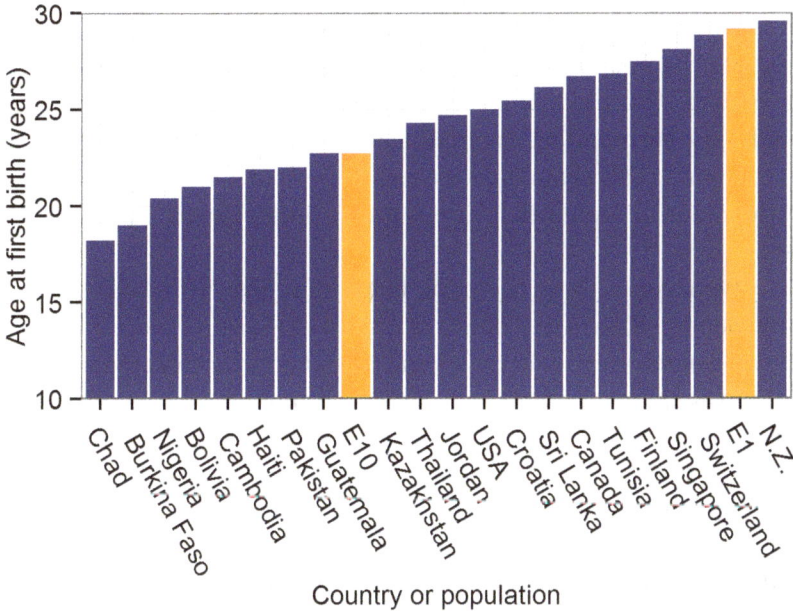

Figure 1.1 Mean ages at first birth for women from a number of countries, and for White British women living the most affluent decile of English neighbourhoods (E1), and the most deprived decile of English neighbourhoods (E10). Data are reproduced from Nettle (2011b) and Nettle (2010a). NZ: New Zealand. Image © Daniel Nettle, CC BY.

Another connection between social gradients and prosocial behaviour comes from the fact that social gradients are not completely reducible to individual characteristics. Social scientists distinguish between an individual's personal socioeconomic position, as measured by things like his income, educational qualifications and employment status, and the deprivation of the area in which he lives, which relates to the average income, education and employment of people in the surrounding locality. It is quite hard to tease apart statistically which is more important in social gradients, personal socioeconomic position (e.g. being poor oneself) or area deprivation (e.g. living in neighbourhood where many other people are poor). This is because the population of Britain is strongly assorted by income, so that most people living in neighbourhoods with many poor people are themselves poor. The best evidence suggests, though, that for many gradients, there is an effect of area-level deprivation above and beyond the effects of individual socioeconomic position (Ludwig et al., 2012; Pickett & Pearl, 2001; Sampson, Morenoff, & Gannon-Rowley, 2002). That is, there are consequences for one's health and behaviour of living surrounded by poor people, above and beyond the consequences of being poor oneself. This must imply that our experience of what *others* in the immediately surrounding environment are doing is important for our own outcomes. This again links us back to social behaviour; indeed to the very definition of social behaviour as things people do that have effects on others.

My twin concerns with social behaviour and with socioeconomic deprivation were allied to a desire to get out of the office more. I had been doing epidemiological work for several years, and what this amounted to in practice was sitting in front of a computer. Although the scientific payoffs for desk work are often considerable, its capacity to expand personal horizons is limited: there is nothing quite like the messy improvisation of a primary empirical project for changing the way you think about the world. I thus decided—after considerable inspiration and advice from my friend Tom Dickins of Middlesex University—to undertake a systematic field study of two contrasting neighbourhoods within Newcastle, one very deprived and the other more affluent. The study aimed to be both ethnographic and ethnological. It would be ethnographic since it aimed to document, in detail, what life was like in the two study neighbourhoods. It would be ethnological, since I wanted to systematically compare the two, and try to explain why they might differ in the ways they did. I dubbed the project the Tyneside Neighbourhoods Project, partly as an homage to David Sloan Wilson and Dan O'Brien's Binghamton Neighborhood Project in upstate New York (Wilson, O'Brien, & Sesma, 2009). The Tyneside Neighbourhoods Project ended up gathering data about many things, such as health behaviour, psychological wellbeing, and plans for the future. However, there was a core running through it that specifically concerned social relationships, social behaviour, and the cognition that underlies them. It is this core that forms the subject matter of this book.

About this book

I should say something at this point about what this book represents and how it is presented. The Tyneside Neighbourhoods Project started out as one study, but went on to spawn a series of linked follow-up investigations in the same sites. I carried out and wrote up the first study myself, but after that, I was fortunate enough to be able to recruit a series of wonderful collaborators. The ones whose work is discussed here were Agathe Colléony, Rebecca Coyne, Kari Britt Schroeder, Jessica Hill, Ruth Jobling and Gillian Pepper. Later parts of the project were executed and in many instances conceived by one or more of them, aided in some cases by undergraduate students from Newcastle University. I also collaborated on related work with Maria Cockerill of North Tyneside Council, and with Stephanie Clutterbuck and Jean Adams, though that work does not feature so directly here. All this led to a series of over ten papers in academic journals, each authored by a different combination of collaborators and each with a slightly different research question, but all based on fieldwork in Tyneside neighbourhoods.

I faced a difficult dilemma in the authorship of this book. The work presented here is not mine alone. Should I then co-author the book with all of my collaborators? Write it as an edited volume, with each chapter having a different author list? In the end I decided to author it by myself. My reasons for doing so relate to the function of the book. There is something interesting in having so many related datasets, using different methods, from the same places. It is like crossing and re-crossing a landscape from different angles, learning more about it each time. Now that the individual datasets are all published, I want to look at them *in toto* and reflect on the story they tell. This means looking at the whole body of the data from a little further back than is possible within a single academic paper.

Given that the function of the book is to stand back and take an overview, it seemed necessary to author it alone. An overview is necessarily someone's view. Any of my collaborators might have come up with quite different overviews from my own, and it would be hard to corral those into a single coherent story. It would either end up as a book designed by a committee, or with my collaborators having to put their names to things they wouldn't have expressed in the same way. Thus, I have written the *book* myself but on the basis of *studies* that were in many cases led by my collaborators. I will attempt to apportion credit (or, I suppose, blame) for the original studies by naming the key investigators and citing the original papers at appropriate points. Conversely, my collaborators are absolved from all the failings of the book; all opinions, errors, omissions and idiocies that appear in these pages rather than those of the peer-reviewed papers are mine alone.

There are some other things to say about the way this book is written. In my view, the main virtue of the project is the amount of quantitative data we were able to collect (see chapter 2 for more details). I have thus not been shy of presenting data in quite a lot of detail, especially visually (and for those wanting to delve deeper still, the raw data are available via Open Science Framework at https://osf.io/ys7g6).[2] On the other hand, given that the objective is an overall synthesis, readability is paramount. There is nothing more inimical to easy reading than a lot of results from statistical modelling. I have therefore decided not to present any details of inferential statistics in this book. If I claim a difference or association is statistically significant, then this is backed up out of sight by appropriate statistical tests, usually to be found in the relevant published paper.

On a related note, the main text is very light on references to the previous literature, and quite heavy on my own interpretations and musings. I have eschewed an extensive literature review section in favour of mentioning key academic influences as they come up. Again, this relates to the different function of the book from the papers. Each of the published papers has a more thorough, better-referenced introduction, and a more measured and technical discussion. Here, I want to emphasize the story of doing the research as it happened, and I don't want to get caught up in relatively esoteric points of difference between academic theories or traditions. I thus apologize to those scholars whose work I have been informed by but do not here cite explicitly, and also for the vast areas of social science literature of which I provide no adequate review in this book, even though it might be relevant. You can't be nimble at the same time as being exhaustive, and so I have aimed for nimbleness.

In the remainder of this chapter, the next section will introduce the study city, Newcastle upon Tyne. The section after that says a little more about the academic concerns that shaped the project. As I have said, I don't want to review these at length, but it is important to give some explanation for why the project ended up taking the form that it did. In the final section, I outline the broad hypotheses that we had in mind as we set out on the research.

---

2   An archived version of the dataset, preserving the data in the form it was at the time of publication, is available at http://dx.doi.org/10.17605/OSF.IO/W9Z2P

The city context: Newcastle upon Tyne

Newcastle upon Tyne is the central city in the Tyneside conurbation, a major urban area of Northern England that occupies the banks of the river Tyne. The total population of Tyneside is around 900,000, making it the seventh largest population centre in the United Kingdom. Newcastle is an ancient city: the eponymous new castle was built in 1080 as part of the attempts of the Normans to secure—and harry—the North of England, but the city has been continuously inhabited since the Roman settlement of Pons Aelius begun in around AD120. Tyneside is a port. By the Middle Ages it was a major exporter of wool, and, increasingly and importantly, coal. Coal is found abundantly within and around the city, and coal was already being exported from Tyneside as early as 1250. By 1644, when Parliamentarian forces blockaded Newcastle during the English civil war, London's annual coal supply fell from 450,000 tons to 3000.

Coal mining, as well as providing large-scale employment directly, drove industrialization of Tyneside, which during the nineteenth became a major centre for railway engineering, shipbuilding, armaments, and other manufacturing. The city expanded to the West, East and North, and its population swelled with immigrants from Ireland, Scotland, and other parts of England. Adjoining villages were incorporated into the city through the nineteenth and early twentieth centuries, as thousands of terraced homes were built in them for miners and other workers. They became the working-class neighbourhoods of Tyneside. (For a historical ethnography of life in one such neighbourhood in the early twentieth century, see Williamson [1982].)

The post-1945 period saw the beginning of economic decline and deindustrialisation on Tyneside. The last coal mine within the city closed in 1954; the larger mines in the surrounding area several decades later. The major heavy industries, notably shipbuilding, also declined through the 1970s and 1980s. Thus, the principal sources of employment that communities had grown up around employed many fewer people or disappeared. New sources of employment developed, notably in services, government-sector jobs and in education, and many parts of the city have regained and surpassed their former prosperity. However, this growth has been spatially uneven. As a result, architecturally and historically fairly similar neighbourhoods in different parts of the city have taken very divergent trajectories. This can be seen clearly by mapping the Index of Multiple Deprivation, the UK government's preferred measure of social deprivation, for Newcastle's constituent census tracts (Figure

1.2). As the map shows, the city contains many areas that are in the 50th-100th percentile when all of England's census tracts are ranked from most to least deprived (that is, they are in the less deprived — or most affluent — half), but at the same time, also contains many tracts that are amongst the 10% most deprived. In fact, though the map does not show it, Tyneside has a number of tracts in England's 1% most deprived. In particular, there are concentrations of extreme deprivation — the large nuclei of dark shading — along the riverside to both the West and East of the city centre. These were areas particularly tied to riverside heavy industries that no longer exist. By contrast, the area to the North East of the city centre, away from the river, although only a few kilometres distant from areas of extreme deprivation, is uniformly below median deprivation. The two main study sites for the Tyneside Neighbourhoods Project were one (Neighbourhood A) in the North East of the city, and one (Neighbourhood B) in the West End. I will deal with the choice of these two sites and their specific characteristics in more detail in chapter 2.

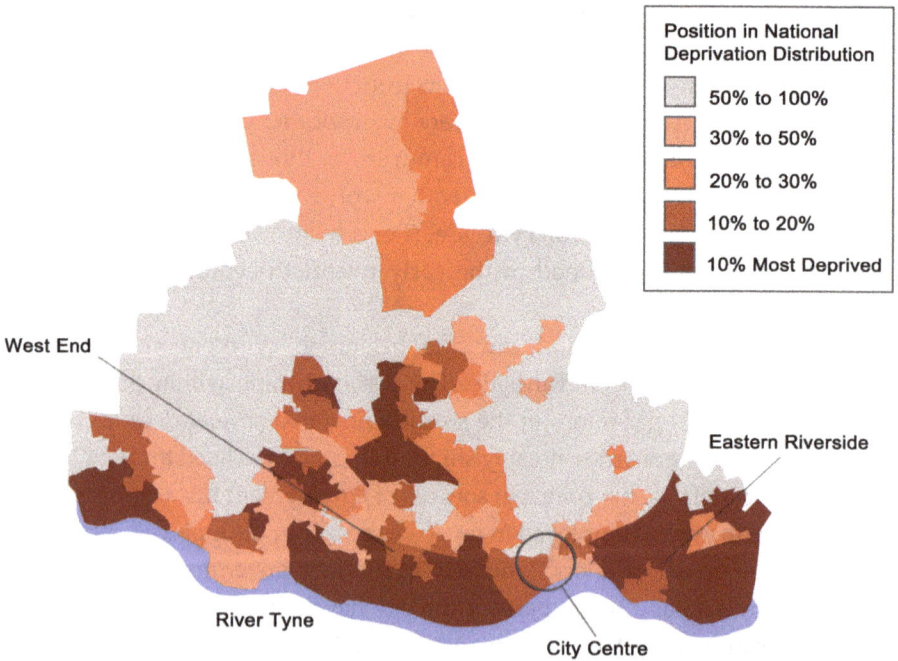

Figure 1.2 A deprivation sketch map of Newcastle upon Tyne. The map is based on the 2010 English Indices of Deprivation. © Jason Zampol, CC BY.

A very large housing-cost gulf developed between the North East of the city and the areas along the riverside. The deprived nuclei were characterized by a long-term pattern of underemployment, economic insecurity and physical dilapidation. This was accompanied by demographic loss; in the West End, for example, the population has declined by around one third over the last few decades (Robinson, 2005). The deprived areas developed negative reputations locally, fuelling a vicious cycle of further outmigration by those with economic options, increasing concentration of economic disadvantage, and a general sense of decline. In the words of one authority on the city's development:

[The West End's] reputation is legendary [...]. One small, telling example of this reputation that I have experienced is of officials going to a meeting in the West End trying to avoid taking their own cars. Another example, illustrating the impacts of the image, is that people in the West End say that employers and others discriminate against them by association, simply because of their address or postcode [...]. Discrimination and the area's reputation encourage those who can do so to leave. Indeed, it has been disconcerting for those running regeneration projects to find that if people are helped to get jobs they are inclined to move out. It doesn't help that the image seems to be starkly and graphically emphasised by the visual reality. Nowadays, there are parts of the West End that look appalling, with boarded up and burnt out houses, cleared sites, barbed wire and shuttered shops (Robinson, 2005).

The problems of deindustrialisation were further exacerbated by mortgage lenders applying no-lending policies to the deprived parts of the city. This further cut the already low value of housing, and restricted the pool of potential residents further still. It was essentially a signal of no confidence in these communities continuing to exist at all.

The deprived parts of the city have been the site of many different urban regeneration initiatives funded by local and national government (non-exhaustive list for the West End; 1960s: Urban Aid; 1970s: Benwell Community Development Programme; 1980s: Tyneside Enterprise Zone; 1990s: West End City Challenge, North Benwell New Beginnings, Scotswood Regeneration, Reviving the Heart of the West End, New Deal for Newcastle West). The most recent initiatives in the West End stem from the 1999 *Going for Growth* plan, and have involved large-scale demolition of housing, with a view to creating communities afresh, attracting people not currently willing to live there. The fieldwork described in this book was carried out in the period after much of the large-scale demolition envisaged by *Going for Growth* had been carried out, but before much of the new housing had been built. The West End made for an eerie sight through this period. In parts of Benwell, streets with street lighting were still there, but they had no houses on them. The former neighbourhood of Scotswood was a huge fallow field, with rocks blocking the ways in and, tall, angular CCTV-camera towers poking through the long, poppy-filled grass. Even the streets had been taken up. The Scotswood site is now (2015) being filled with the first houses of the new neighbourhood messianically named *The Rise*. Elsewhere, new housing is complete and already being occupied.

Neighbourhood B of this study consists of streets in the West End that were not demolished, and were not due to be. They were still fully functional and the houses largely inhabited. However, it should be borne in mind that the fieldwork was carried out at a particular moment in time: a moment when people in Neighbourhood B had endured many years of uncertainty about the future of the whole area, had seen many areas around them destroyed, and had not as yet seen much new put into the empty spaces that surrounded them. It is impossible to say, though interesting to ask, how different our results would have been had our study been done five years later, just as it is interesting to wonder what they would have been like if it had been done fifty or seventy years earlier, when the West End was still poor, but the basis of its economic life was very different.

Motivations for the Tyneside Neighbourhoods Project

The idea of studying in detail the social life of one or more urban neighbourhoods is by no means a new one. The project fits in some respects rather closely into the empirical tradition known as community studies in sociology (for a review of this area, see Crow & Allan, 1994). Community studies have often focused on working-class neighbourhoods, including on Tyneside in some cases, and often compared multiple sites in either the same or different cities (see e.g. Byrne, 1989). The present project shared the goals of some classic community studies, in that we wished to systematically describe, in our study neighbourhoods, the informal social relationships and interactions that make up so much of everyday life. (Strictly speaking, it would be better to call it a location study rather than a community study, since the study units were defined geographically and we cannot assume *a priori* that they necessarily function as communities.) However, my background is not in sociology, and I admit I was poorly acquainted with the community studies tradition of research at the time of setting out—so much so that some of the similarities of the Tyneside Neighbourhoods Project to the studies in that tradition represent lucky convergence rather than inheritance. The idea of studying different neighbourhoods within the same city nonetheless attracted me, because it seemed to relate to several broader theoretical issues that cut right across the social and behavioural sciences. The first of these is one I have already touched upon: the issue of scale of variation in human social behaviour.

Through the 2000s, a series of studies had shown quantitatively that measures of social behaviour varied across cultures (Henrich et al., 2005; Henrich, Ensminger, McElreath, & Barr, 2010; Herrmann, Thöni, & Gächter, 2008). 'Cultures' here almost always meant either countries or ethnic groups, and the measures were either surveys or the monetary dilemmas known as economic games that we will discuss in more detail in chapter 2. These studies were important in showing that you could not make simple generalizations about whether humans were or were not cooperative; you needed to specify which humans you were talking about. In a way, though, these studies were not the most striking demonstration possible of the extraordinary flexibility of human behaviour. The kinds of groups compared in this body of research differed in so many ways—their natural environment, their mode of subsistence, their level of economic development, their monetary and political systems, their languages—that you really ought to expect them to differ on measures of social behaviour. It is surprising that they did not differ even more. The proportion of variation explained by country or ethnic group in these studies was fairly modest: though the group differences were statistically significant, there was always much more variation within groups than between (Bell, Richerson, & McElreath, 2009; Henrich et al., 2012). The ethnic group has long been a privileged level of analysis in anthropological thought, and there is lively discussion in the literature on the extent to which this is justified (Henrich et al., 2012; Lamba & Mace, 2011, Morin 2015). To sort out the relative magnitudes of within-society and between-society variation requires what is called a multi-level study, where you have data from many individuals from many social groups from many societies. We weren't going to be able to do that by conducting an ethnographic study within one city. However, we would be able to quantify between-neighbourhood differences and compare their magnitude to those seen between ethnic groups in cross-cultural studies using similar methodologies.

Another reason that a neighbourhood study was attractive relates to the distinction in social science between macro and micro studies. Macro studies are of the kind we have already discussed: they look at group averages in outcome across broad entities like countries or regions, often relating the variation in those averages to variation in some group-level predictor variable, either historical or contemporaneous. These studies are important because they reveal consequential differences between human social groups. One of the striking results of macro studies in the field of social behaviour has been to show that cultural differences can be rather stable over the long term. For example, there are marked differences between different parts of the USA in terms of the use of interpersonal violence. People in some areas are more prone than people in others to use violence to defend personal reputation, the so-called culture of honour (Nisbett, 1993). The prevalence of culture-of-honour violence in a county today, at least within the Southern states, can be traced right back to that county's pattern of lawlessness and violence in the eighteenth century (Grosjean, 2014). These historical differences still show an influence when you control for current economic factors, and although the homogenizing influences of contemporary US life have lessened them over time, they have not yet abolished them completely. This suggests that once certain cultural patterns are set in, they become self-sustaining, and can persist over many generations of individuals, and much change in the current ecology. Such a conclusion sits well with a view of humans as 'cultural beings', the view traditional in much of anthropology. Under this view, people help or harm each other in particular ways because they are acculturated in societies that have historical traditions of helping or marking each other in those ways. These cultural traditions have their own inertia and dynamics that decouple them at least to some extent from subsequent changes in the ecology. (I am not claiming, by the way, that all macro studies necessarily lead us to view humans as cultural beings, only that some macro studies produce data easily interpreted from this perspective.)

At the opposite extreme from macro studies are micro studies. Here, the units of analysis are individual people, and researchers explore, often experimentally, the immediate causal factors that underlie their decisions. In the field of social behaviour, for example, there has been a lot of experimental work looking at what kinds of contexts produce cooperative behaviour and what kinds do not. Some of this work is done in the laboratory. In one famous set of studies, people were formed up into artificial social groups in which they were invited to contribute to a common pool resource that would benefit them all (Fehr & Gachter, 2000). In one experimental condition, the players had no possible way of sanctioning other group members who did not contribute. In this condition, predictably, contributions declined over time and the common pool resource ended up poorly funded. The experimenters changed the rules so that people had a way of sanctioning non-contributors. With this change in place, contributions to the common pool resource increased immediately, and remained high over time. In fact, people did not even need to directly experience being sanctioned to change their contributions; they saw that the possible consequences were different, and recalibrated their behaviour accordingly.

Other micro studies of social behaviour have been done in the field. Perhaps the most impressive example is experiments by Keizer, Lindenberg and Steg (2008). In city streets in the Netherlands, the researchers introduced, on some days, subtle cues of disorder into the environment. These cues included graffiti, or bicycles locked to a fence in violation of a rule. They showed that on days when disorder cues were present, people were much more likely to drop litter themselves, take a prohibited shortcut, or even pocket someone else's €5, than on days when those cues were absent. The effects were large. The difference between denizens of the Dutch cities on a day when there is graffiti in the environment those same Dutch citizens on a day when there is no graffiti is at least as big as the largest between-population differences in social behaviour that have been observed in macro studies.

The strength of micro studies is that they provide insight into causal processes underlying individual behavioural decisions. Perhaps the most striking generalization arising from micro studies of social behaviour, and exemplified by Keizer et al.'s results, is that people's social behaviour is enormously influenced by immediate context. You can really change what people do by even a small manipulation of their environment, and you can do this in real time. This sits well with the view of humans as 'agentic beings' that is characteristic of economics amongst other disciplines. Under this view, people are able to respond strategically to the incentives and opportunities of their local context: change the environment, and people's behaviour will follow suit. There is an interesting tension between thinking of humans as cultural beings and thinking of them as agentic beings: on the one hand, the long-term stability of macro patterns, suggesting social culture has its own independent transmission and inertia; on the other hand, the strategic flexibility of individual people, suggesting that social behaviour is an immediate strategic response to current context.

In truth humans are beings that are both cultural and agentic, and one of the most interesting challenges in the behavioural sciences is constructing detailed explanations of particular behaviours that do justice to both components. Individuals are indeed flexible and strategic, as the micro-experiments demonstrate. They certainly don't have a fixed, inherited cultural formula that they follow slavishly regardless of current context. On the other hand, there really are—at least sometimes—long-term cultural traditions (Morin 2015). These exist because people in populations influence one another. The behavioural output from one person forms part of the environmental input to which his neighbours may respond, creating the potential for a cycle of transmission. Under certain conditions, the aggregate behaviour can end up stable over long periods of time, even though all the individual people are capable of behaving flexibly and strategically.

The idea of a neighbourhoods project appealed because it was at a meso-scale, offering some of the opportunities of a macro study and some of those of a micro study. It shared with macro studies the possibility of identifying group-level average differences; particular neighbourhoods have reputations for particular social cultures, and these can last for many years. On the other hand, neighbourhoods are small enough and similar enough to one another that you can drill down deeply into exactly what individual perceptions or experiences are driving any neighbourhood differences in behaviour. It might even be possible in one or two instances to use the experimental method, deliberately manipulating the experiences or cues that people receive, to catch the workings of the decision-making processes underlying people's prosocial and antisocial acts, and thus potentially understanding the proximate determinants of a neighbourhood's social traditions. The meso-scale thus seemed a fruitful terrain on which to try to reconcile the cultural and agentic aspects of variation in social behaviour.

The Tyneside Neighbourhoods Project thus aimed to examine within-society variation, to work at the meso-scale, and to explore the roles of both individual decision-making and cultural transmission in maintaining patterns of behaviour. It had another aspiration, which was to use multiple quantitative methods, with equal emphasis on the multiple and on the quantitative. The reasons for this aspiration, and the methods it led us to develop, will be laid out in chapter 2.

Competing narratives:
Kropotkin versus the Mountain People

One of the reasons it seemed interesting to study social behaviour in an affluent and a deprived community is that there were two venerable traditions of thought available to us that led to exactly opposite expectations about what patterns we should see. These traditions are too diffuse to be called hypotheses; they are really alternative framing narratives about deprivation and social life that scholars and commentators are recurrently drawn to. I shall call them, for reasons that will become clear below, the Kropotkin narrative and the Mountain People narrative.

Piotr Kropotkin, the great nineteenth-century polymath and anarchist thinker, spent long periods travelling in Siberia and Manchuria. He observed the terrible harshness of the environment, and the consequent precariousness of life for the animals and plants. What impressed him, though, was how individuals cooperated as a strategy for survival. Whether it was the hunting packs of carnivores, the breeding colonies and flocks of birds, or the family groups of small mammals, Kropotkin argued that the way individuals coped with environmental difficulties was by developing mutually-beneficial social relationships. Kropotkin argued from the outset that this observation should be as applicable for understanding human societies as it was for animal ones.

An accurate reading of Kropotkin's book *Mutual Aid* (1902) would not be that cooperative relationships emerge only in harsh environments. Rather, Kropotkin saw cooperative relationships as a ubiquitous component of how individuals manage to survive under *all* circumstances. However, harsh environments did allow you to see the importance of mutual aid particularly clearly. For this reason, his name has become perennially attached to the idea that harsh environments foster prosociality (Smaldino, Schank, & McElreath, 2013). Within a contemporary developed country like Britain, 'harsher' can be roughly equated to 'more socioeconomically deprived'.

For our study, then, if we began with the Kropotkin narrative in mind, we would expect that it would be in our deprived study site where informal prosocial behaviours would be most strongly expressed. Individual financial resources are scarcer in such communities. The financial returns on labour tend to be much lower, even where formal employment is available, and consequently people's ability to purchase market solutions to their problems is generally weak. They have to find ways of coping with this difficult constellation of circumstances, and under the Kropotkinian view, they will do this by turning to, and investing in, informal prosocial relationships within their neighbourhoods. Their social relationships will be particularly strong, and they will use their social networks for mounting cooperative solutions to their economic difficulties.

You can certainly find empirical evidence easily read into framework of the Kropotkin narrative. Young and Willmott's famous community study *Family and Kinship in East London* (1957) depicted a working-class life of numerous social bonds beyond the household, neighbourliness, mutual aid and communal solidarity. Subsequent community studies of other working-class areas reinforced this basic view. More recently, in a series of psychological studies, Paul K. Piff and colleagues have found that young Americans of lower socioeconomic position tend to be more generous towards others, and more prosocially oriented, than their higher-socioeconomic-status peers (Côté, Piff, & Willer, 2013; Piff, Kraus, Côté, Cheng, & Keltner, 2010; Piff, 2014). This seems to be largely driven by their being more empathetic and compassionate, and more strongly endorsing egalitarian principles: we are all in this together.

However, the authority of some of this evidence is contested. Young and Willmott have been heavily criticized for relying on rather narrow, at times impressionistic, sources of data, and hence, perhaps, seeing what it suited them to see (Crow & Allan, 1994; Day, 2006). Follow-up studies in the very same localities saw much more conflict and isolation (Cornwell, 1984; Holme, 1985). Reliance on participants' public accounts had produced a much more positive view of social life than the disturbing concerns people would raise when asked in private (Cornwell, 1984). This led to widespread scholarly questioning of the romantic Young-and-Wilmott depiction, as well as of the methods that generated it. The barbed comment that the community study is the sociologist's substitute for the novel is widely reproduced (Crow & Allan, 1994 p. xii; Day, 2006 p. 29), and seems to have these portrayals of working-class life in mind. Note that the critiques of Young and Willmott do not necessarily apply to the more recent work of Piff and colleagues, whose methods are very different. Nonetheless, they do remind us that we should enter the enquiry with appropriate scepticism about the Kropotkin narrative as it applies to urban deprivation.

In the opposite corner from the Kropotkin narrative is the narrative I will associate with Colin Turnbull's ethnographic monograph *The*

Mountain People (Turnbull, 1972). *The Mountain People* was written following fieldwork amongst the Ik people of Northern Uganda carried out at a time in the 1960s when drought had led to very severe famine. Turnbull describes a situation where all prosocial norms had basically collapsed; people were, in Turnbull's words 'unfriendly, uncharitable, inhospitable and generally mean' (p. 32). People were so desperate they could focus only on trying to survive themselves. The elderly died first; children were left to fend for themselves and died second; husbands fed themselves at the expense of their wives and vice versa; the dying were abandoned or stolen from. People actively avoided creating social relationships, because of the obligations they create and the obvious difficulties of having to deal with desperate individuals. Turnbull argued that under these circumstances, there was nothing in Ik villages that could be described as social structure, and no norms or rules of conduct that could be thought of as social. All that went on was the struggle of each person to survive: the Ik 'place the individual good above all else and almost demand that each get away with as much as he can' (p. 101). The pervasive interpersonal attitudes were mistrust and fear, and the closest of neighbours were mistrusted and feared the most (p. 134).

In invoking *The Mountain People* to give a name to a narrative, it is important to be clear about what I am and am not implying. Firstly, I am not implying that Turnbull's ethnography was in fact a veridical representation of Ik social life at that time. The evidential basis of this work, too, has been criticized (Beidelman, 1973). Indeed, Bernd Heine reported a couple of decades later that some of the Ik were interested in the possibility of taking legal action against Turnbull for his misrepresentation of them (Heine, 1985). Second, I am not invoking or endorsing Turnbull's view in the book that Ik society was irreparably broken and it would be better if it died out (p. 285). His proposal that the Ik should be broken up into small groups, forcibly relocated, and integrated into other communities round the rest of the country (pp. 283-84), is shockingly autocratic to modern sensibilities, though it is oddly reminiscent of occasional think-tank proposals for what to do with deprived inner-city areas in the North of England. Finally, I am not proposing too literal a similarity between the situation of the Ik and that of deprived parts of Newcastle today. Some similarity there is, since the shadow of hunger is not unknown in the West End of Newcastle. An emergency-assistance food bank opened there in 2013. According to its website, on the day before it closed for the Christmas break at the end of 2014, it provided food parcels to 1057 people. In September 2015, in an incident that could have come straight out of the pages of *The Mountain People*, it was broken into and all the food stored in it stolen. Nonetheless, the dissimilarities between the two contexts are obviously profound.

What I wish to extract from *The Mountain People* is a central intuition. This intuition is that deprivation undermines prosociality, because people are so preoccupied by just getting by that cooperating with others is something they can ill afford to think about. Note how the logic of the *Mountain People* narrative is an inversion of Kropotkin's. In the Kropotkinian world, having good social relationships is so fundamental to survival that only bourgeois decadence would allow it to be forgotten; when things get tough, that is when you will see prosociality most clearly. By contrast, in the world of the Mountain People, the foremost and obligatory thing you need to do is to get by yourself. Investing in social relationships is something you will want to do once the more basic individual wants have been secured, like one of the higher-level needs in Maslow's famous needs hierarchy. When times are hard, prosociality will be driven from the landscape. As Turnbull put it:

> It seems that, far from being basic human qualities, [prosocial tendencies] are superficial luxuries we can afford in times of plenty [...]. Given the situation in which the Ik found themselves [...] man has not time for such luxuries, and a much more basic man appears, using much more basic survival tactics (Turnbull, 1972 p. 32).

For the present case, if we begin our enquiries with the Mountain People narrative in our minds, we will expect that in Neighbourhood B, where relative poverty and economic insecurity are widespread, people will be much more focused on individual subsistence, and hence prosocial behaviour will be less in evidence than in Neighbourhood A. You can find empirical support for this expectation, too. Haushofer (2013) marshalled an impressive amount of evidence from a dataset called the World Values Survey, comprising responses from over one hundred thousand respondents in 43 countries. He showed that within each country, there was a social gradient in trust, and in a measure of prosociality. (The prosociality measure asked about helping family members rather than people in general.) Trust and prosociality were highest in the richest decile of income, a little lower in the ninth decile, lower still in the eighth, and so on, with the poorest decile reporting themselves the least trusting and the least inclined to help. The gradients were strikingly steep and smooth. Interestingly, Haushofer found that the between-country differences in trust and prosociality were largely extensions of the individual-level patterns. That is, poorer *countries* were on average less trusting and less prosocial than richer ones, just as poorer individuals within a country were on average less trusting and less prosocial than richer ones.

Which narrative do we choose, the Kropotkin or the Mountain People? It is not necessarily an either/or choice. It is simplistic to reduce prosociality to a single axis and predict that there will be either 'more' or 'less' of it in one neighbourhood than another. A more nuanced expectation would be that prosocial behaviour will be present in both of our study neighbourhoods, but will take different forms, and perhaps encounter different obstacles. The two narratives are therefore only that: framing devices we can keep in our minds as we begin to examine, in chapters 3 and 4, what the datasets actually tell us.

2. Study sites and methods

I tried to get away, but I couldn't get far,
'Cos a man with a tow-truck repossessed my car.

This chapter describes the main study sites, discusses how the methods were chosen and developed, and provides an overview of the datasets that were generated in the course of the Tyneside Neighbourhoods Project.

The study neighbourhoods

I chose Neighbourhoods A and B as the main study sites after some archival research and a number of informal visits. Very extensive social and economic data are available for census areas within the UK. The most convenient size of census tract, the Lower Super Output Area, is a little small for a neighbourhood study, and in Newcastle, the neighbourhoods as recognized by local people tend to be cut in pieces by Lower Super Output Area boundaries. Thus, I decided that each of the study neighbourhoods would consist of two adjoining Lower Super Output Areas that together roughly corresponded to a neighbourhood as recognized and named by residents. All census and other third-party statistics given for the study neighbourhoods given in this book have been created by taking a summation or population-weighted average of the figures for the constituent Lower Super Output Areas. The two Lower Super Output Areas making up each study neighbourhood are pretty similar to each other on most indices.

The search strategy was to find two neighbourhoods that were as far as possible similar in every respect except the level of deprivation. Of course, deprivation changes a lot of things: the state of the properties, the shops

 http://dx.doi.org/10.11647/OBP.0084.02

present, the types of food available and many other things are different in deprived and in affluent neighbourhoods. Thus, the neighbourhoods would inevitably differ in myriad ways. The search was thus not for an exact match, but rather for two studies where everything that *could* be similar given contrasting economic fortunes was similar, and the differences were as far as possible related to socioeconomic deprivation, rather than extraneous factors.

I selected a site in the North East of the city for Neighbourhood A, and in the West End for Neighbourhood B. The sites selected were satisfactory in a number of ways. They were about the same distance (3km) from the city centre. Each consisted of a recognizable main street with a supermarket or two and a selection of smaller shops and food outlets. The main street ran North-South in one case, and East-West in the other. Leaving the main street in both perpendicular directions were residential streets; these led to networks of other residential streets and then to the neighbourhood boundaries. Both neighbourhoods were generally low-rise and contained a great deal of housing around or slightly more than one hundred years old, much of it terraced. Beyond this there were some differences, such as a greater number of large detached houses in Neighbourhood A, and a greater number of smaller post-1945 houses and flats in Neighbourhood B, although there were some of these in Neighbourhood A too. In neither neighbourhood were the residents mainly students. Students are a very particular population, high in individual socioeconomic status, but with no long-term ties or investment in the community, and comparing a student to a non-student population would be misleading. On the whole, it was possible to imagine without too much a stretch that if economic fortunes improved, Neighbourhood B would start to look rather like Neighbourhood A does now, and, if the economy collapsed, Neighbourhood A would start to look somewhat like B does now.

The neighbourhood statistics backed up how good the match was (Table 1.1). The population sizes were about the same. The population structure differed in predictable ways (proportionately fewer men and more children in Neighbourhood B), but the differences were slight. The median age was only slightly higher in Neighbourhood A. You will notice that the number of households is rather larger in Neighbourhood B. This is because in Neighbourhood B, half of households with children contain only a lone adult, whereas in Neighbourhood A, the great majority of households with children (88%) contain two adults (Nettle, 2011a). This is itself an interesting pattern to which we will return.

Table 1.1 Key statistics for the two study neighbourhoods. Data are reproduced from Nettle (2011a), and the ultimate sources are the 2001 census and 2004 indices of multiple deprivation.

	Neighbourhood A	Neighbourhood B
Total population	3098	3223
Males	1502 (48.5%)	1508 (46.8%)
Under-16s	708 (22.9%)	810 (25.1%)
Median age	37	34.5
Households	1250	1589
Percentage population born in UK	92	92
Index of Multiple Deprivation	8.74	76.43
Index of Multiple Deprivation percentile	79th	1st

Particularly important for the conception of the study was the fact that the ethnic composition of the two sites was very similar, with both study sites containing, at the 2001 census, 92% people born in the UK. Thus, whatever else the study was doing, it would not predominantly be comparing the behaviour of different ethnic groups, or immigrants to non-immigrants. An important caveat is in order here, which is that there has been considerable immigration into Neighbourhood B in the years since the 2001 census. The data from the 2011 census, which were not available at the beginning of the study, have now been released, and the percentage UK-born for Neighbourhood B is now closer to 70% (Hill, Jobling, Pollet, & Nettle, 2014). Thus, it remains the case that we are comparing two predominantly British-born white communities, but the difference in the number of immigrants should be noted.

If the upper rows of Table 1.1 show statistics that are similar across the two neighbourhoods, the lower rows show the opposite. The Index of Multiple Deprivation is a composite statistic on an arbitrary scale, so values of 9 and 76 will not mean much out of context. The percentages are more informative: these show that if all of England's 34,000-odd Lower Super Output Areas were laid out from the most to least deprived, the areas making up Neighbourhood A would be found around position 27,000. The areas making up Neighbourhood B would lie in the first few hundred. In the Tyneside context, Neighbourhood A is about as affluent as it gets whilst still remaining within the city, whilst Neighbourhood B is typical of the concentrations of deprivation in the West End and Eastern riverside of the city.

A more dramatic way of seeing the difference comes from the UK government's Neighbourhood Statistics website. The idea of this site is that residents or potential house buyers can enter a postcode and obtain a dashboard of useful statistics about the area around that particular street. Central to these is a handy visual aid: the meter of deprivation. As Figure 2.1 shows, the meter of deprivation looks pretty healthy for a postcode in the middle of Neighbourhood A, but it is maxed out for a postcode in Neighbourhood B. Quite what the creators of this web site were planning to do for neighbourhood regeneration, or whether they had thought about the possible adverse consequences, I am not sure.

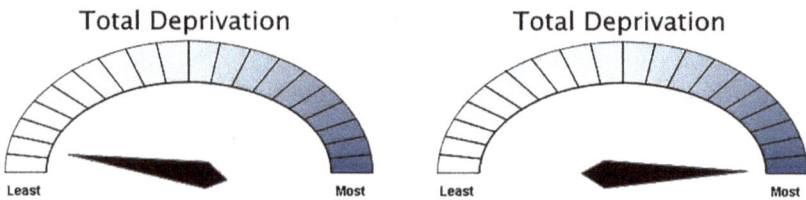

Figure 2.1 The meter of deprivation for an address in Neighbourhood A (left) and one in Neighbourhood B (right). Image from http://www.neighbourhood.statistics.gov.uk, subject to the terms of the Open Government Licence.

It is important to be clear about what the design of the Tyneside Neighbourhoods Project does and does not allow us to claim. It looks rather like a quasi-experimental design: two sites that are the same, except that fate has assigned one of them to socioeconomic deprivation. Thus, any differences in behaviour that we see between them tell us what the causal consequences of deprivation are, clean of other confounding variables. This seems to me an advance on traditional one-site ethnographies, in that at least there is *one* explicit and systematic comparison. My original conception of the Tyneside Neighbourhoods Projects was indeed as a quasi-experimental comparison along these lines. However, in truth the project does not allow such strong or such general claims.

The reason concerns a basic principle of research design: replication. If we want to conclude something about variation at level X, we need multiple replications of entities at level X. What this means in this case is that to say something general about the consequences of neighbourhood deprivation, we would need multiple pairs of matched neighbourhoods, one in each pair deprived and the other one not deprived. Without such replication, any differences we observe between the two neighbourhoods are interesting but do not necessarily generalize to other affluent-deprived comparisons. They might not be due to deprivation at all, but to some other idiosyncratic feature of one of the sites I happen to have chosen. It might be that what we see in Neighbourhood B is very specifically to do with the uncertainty created by the threat of large-scale demolition, or the historical legacy of heavy industry, or any other specific feature of Neighbourhood B, rather than an epitome of what deprivation always does. Getting more participants in Neighbourhoods A and B to take part does nothing to alleviate this problem. That gives us more replication within our neighbourhoods, but does not increase our generalizability at the neighbourhood level at all. Partly for this reason, a critique of community studies and ethnographies in general is that they are not cumulative: we learn something about another location, but we don't progress toward theory or knowledge of a more general character (Crow & Allan, 1994 p. 195).

I acknowledge this limitation, but do not feel it undermines the value of the data presented here. By studying Neighbourhood B in contrast to Neighbourhood A, we will uncover patterns, generate ideas, and form hypotheses. The same patterns can subsequently be looked for, and the hypotheses tested, across a broader range of places. Some things will turn out to be similar elsewhere, and some will not, but that is an empirically tractable question. Related to this point is our commitment to developing repeatable quantitative measures that could be applied elsewhere to allow for direct comparability, a commitment I discuss in the next section. Moreover, this is not just a study of neighbourhoods, but also a study of humans living in those neighbourhoods. Quite a lot of the data to be presented in this book actually tests hypotheses at the level of the individual person rather than the neighbourhood, since the studies were concerned with understanding the individual-level processes whose emergent consequence was the neighbourhood-level difference. We had plenty of replication at the individual level, since our samples of people were typically quite large.

Development of methods: General considerations

We now had two study sites. What were we going to do in them? There was no off-the-shelf set of standard methodologies. In this section, I discuss some of the general considerations that went into the methods; in the final section of the chapter, I discuss in more detail the individual datasets that we ended up collecting.

Qualitative and quantitative methods

The reporting of the results of ethnographic research in anthropology does not tend to be very quantitative. Community studies in sociology are somewhat more quantitative, but patchily so. By contrast, I felt from early on that in the Tyneside Neighbourhoods Project that I wanted to quantify everything. The neglect of quantification in studies of social life is something of a curiosity, since researchers gather a large amount of data in the course of them, and there are many simple ways that they could use quantification more widely than they typically do. I can only attribute it to a widespread but unhelpful view that there are two different classes of methods, quantitative and qualitative.

If you accept the premise that there are two classes of methods, qualitative and quantitative, then it is easy to see how you end up preferring quantitative methods if you have clearly specified *a priori* hypotheses to test between, but qualitative methods if you want to learn about the experiences of a particular group of people in a rich and open-ended way. However, this argument rests on a false premise, which is that quantitative and qualitative methods are mutually exclusive classes. In fact, *all* methods in the social and behavioural sciences are qualitative. This is because they all involve decisions about what to ask, what to record, how to represent and encode the data, and what the typology of outcomes is. These are fundamentally qualitative decisions, regardless of whether or not you go on to count the occurrences you have decided are significant. So, to the extent there is a choice of methods, it is between qualitative data that are represented numerically, and qualitative data that are excerpted or summarized verbally or visually.

Faced with this choice, it is my view that you can get more from the data, and allow the data to speak more, if you attempt to quantify the entities or occurrences you are interested in. It is true that any particular quantification you do loses some of the information in the underlying data. However, so does any verbal summary, thematic analysis, or representative quotation. Using numbers versus not using numbers does not make any difference to this. Non-quantitative analyses are generally less transparent in terms of what encoding and editing processes have gone on than quantitative analyses are. With a well-presented quantitative analysis, filtering of the data has occurred, but at least the reader has some hope of understanding what kind of filtering it was. As for open-endedness, the important issue is not whether you quantify or not, but whether you can return to the underlying raw data and re-encode them differently if you have some new insight, idea or question. My personal experience has been that through trying to get substantial-sized samples and pull out numbers from them, I have often seen things that I did not expect and even ran counter to my phenomenological impressions. I don't know if the same would have happened if I had not forced myself through the imperfect but self-improving discipline of quantification.

Quantification of results, if coupled to explicitly described data-collection methods, has the potential to enhance the generalizability of social research and make the knowledge it produces more cumulative. Instead of merely noting that things are different in our study site than that of another study, we can take the same measures, compare the data, and test statistically where the similarities and differences lie. Quantification is also potentially useful for the legitimation of ethnography. Ethnographers make generalizations of record about the behaviour and experiences of particular groups of people at particular times. Sometimes, quite properly, those generalizations are contested. We have already met two cases of this in chapter 1: Young and Willmott (1957) and Turnbull (1972). Such contestations can quickly descend into one person's anecdote against another's, and that means we need to know the basis of each party's claims. Quantification, in tandem with adequate description of sampling methods, can help here. Yes, you saw X happen, but how many observation bouts did you make in which X could have happened, and during how many of them did it actually happen? Quantification does not of course guarantee that all the generalizations we make will be fair or uncontroversial. I have come to appreciate through this project how every measure has multiple possible interpretations, and often raises as many questions as it answers. At least with quantification, though, we know how the generalizations were arrived at, and that can be the starting point for a dialogue between views.

Thus, I decided early on that though the Tyneside Neighbourhoods Project was ineluctably a qualitative endeavour, nothing was to be admissible as evidence unless a number could be put on it. It was an essay in quantitative ethnography, and the methods for quantitative ethnography (or as I would prefer it, the quantitative methods for ethnography), are still fragmentary (Efferson, Takezawa, & McElreath, 2007). Thus, we were going to have to invent, borrow and adapt a range of assays, sampling strategies and coding schemes, to which I will turn shortly.

Direct observation and self-report

Alongside the commitment to quantification sat a commitment to multiple methods. In particular, a prominent role would be assigned to direct observation of behaviour (also known as systematic social observation). Direct, systematic observation of behaviour is strangely little used in contemporary social science, although there was more done back in the 1950s than there is now. As Payne and Payne (2004 p. 157) drily put it: 'People coming new to social research are often surprised to learn that social scientists […] do not use observation very much as a method'. This is all the more puzzling since anthropology, for example, prides itself on its detailed characterization of human life at relatively small and fine scales. Direct behavioural observation avoids recruitment bias (people who choose to participate being atypical of the population from which they are drawn), avoids demand characteristics (people behaving differently because they know they are taking part in a study), is faithful to life because it *is* part of life, and allows for almost limitless detail in what is recorded. Ethnographers do, of course, do a great deal of informal social observation. They just don't tend to systemize it or turn it into structured quantitative data. The neglect of direct behavioural observation is not restricted to anthropology; it is underused in psychology too (Baumeister, Vohs, & Funder, 2007; Furr, 2009), and there is been a suggestion that sociologists should use it more to understand neighbourhood effects (Sampson et al., 2002).

There are some weak reasons for the under-use of direct behavioural observation, and some more defensible ones. The weakest reasons are pragmatic: direct observation is time-intensive—for data capture, transcription and processing—and often just harder work than other methods, whereas researchers want usable data quickly and cheaply. The strong conformity-preserving features of the academic system mean that once direct observation is rare, it tends to remain rare. Researchers want their studies to look like the other studies they read in the literature, and peer reviewers enforce this. This conformity has good aspects, such as increasing the possibility of replication and cumulation, but bad aspects, such as imposing a rare-type disadvantage on methodological innovations that would be genuinely useful.

The most defensible reason for the neglect of direct behavioural observation is that observation tells us little or nothing about the cognition or goals of the people involved. Max Weber gave the example of seeing a man chopping wood: from observing him, we cannot necessarily tell if he is doing wage labour, stocking his hearth, or just enjoying some exercise.

To gain insight into this, you need to ask him; hence the centrality of questionnaires and interviews in social science. This is a good point but incomplete as it stands. To understand a man's chopping of wood, it may not be sufficient to observe that he chops it, but it is necessary. He might not actually chop wood, even when he claims he does. There can be important and systematic gaps between what people do and what they say they do. Thus, even if our research interest is in the subjective meaning of the wood-chopping, we should use multiple methods, including a naturalistic observation component. Without this component, our picture of people's lives is incomplete in a fundamental way. In a prefatory passage, Young and Willmott (1957 p. xxxi) warn the reader that 'for the most part, we can only report what people say they do, which is not necessarily the same as what they actually do'. Yet what people actually do would seem to be a fairly central aspect of the enquiry. Thus, I determined early on that we would gather as many different kinds of data as we could, but that recording what people actually do in Neighbourhoods A and B would form a central plank of the research. Some of the most interesting insights came at the moments where the self-report and behavioural data pointed in opposite directions, as we shall see.

My desire to give direct behavioural observation a central role was no doubt influenced by the fact that I also do research in animal behaviour, where for obvious reasons direct observation looms much larger. However, there was also a social science influence, coming from the urban studies of people like William H. Whyte. (William H. Whyte is not to be confused with his unrelated contemporary William Foote Whyte, also a social researcher. William Foote wrote a famous ethnography called *Street Corner Society*, which would have been a fine title for William H.'s book *City: Rediscovering the Center.* However, William Foote's methodological approach was actually quite different.) William H. Whyte spent much of his career doing direct behavioural observation of how people actually used city environments, such as sidewalks and plazas, particularly in New York. Whyte's work stands today, despite his—for my taste—insufficient quantification of the very interesting data he and his collaborators gathered. In *City: Rediscovering the Center*, Whyte notes that there were already many studies on how people use cities prior to his. He says:

> Some of the studies were illuminating. Taken together they suffered one deficiency: the research was vicarious; it was once or twice removed from the ultimate reality being studied. That reality was people in everyday situations. That is what we studied. (Whyte, 2009 p. 5).

I feel the same about the contemporary use of questionnaires, surveys, and interviews as social science methods of choice. To the extent that these are taken as assays of people's behaviour, they are vicarious, once or twice removed from the reality they purport to represent. Thus, it is essential to also study directly the ultimate reality of people behaving in everyday situations.

Economic games

Economic games were also part of the plan from early on. Economic games came into prominence particularly in the 1990s and 2000s. They are, in essence, standardized financial decisions. They are always incentivized with real money. Economic games gave economists a way to find out how people actually allocate a scarce resource in a social context, rather than relying on *a priori* assumptions about how an economic agent ought to do so. For example, in the classic Ultimatum Game, one player can propose a split of the stake (say £10) between himself and another player. If the second player accepts the proposed division, they both go away with their share, whereas if the second player rejects it, they both leave with nothing. The players are anonymous from one another and will not interact again. In a world of actors motivated only to maximize their financial gain from the interaction, the first player ought to offer the second player the minimum possible amount from the £10: 1 penny if the money can be broken down that small. The second player ought to accept this, as 1 penny is more than nothing. Thus, we should observe splits favouring the first player as extreme as £9.99 to £0.01.

In fact, this is not the result we typically observe at all. Second players reject low offers, even though they hurt themselves as well as the other player by doing so. First players don't make offers as low as they should — they tend to offer quite a lot. This may be in part due to their understanding that low offers may well get rejected, and they will lose everything. However, they tend to offer more than is necessary to maximize their expected return given how second players actually behave. In other words, rather than maximizing the monetary return from the interaction like economic automata, the players behave like people actually do in social situations, with pride, spite, conscience, and so on. (I will not make a cheap aside about this being a major discovery for economists.)

The first wave of findings from economic games tended to be interpreted in pan-human terms. The game results were held up as showing how *humans* behave, which was often at variance with the way simple economic models suggested they ought to behave. This was of course rather a naïve conclusion, since usually each study was done on a single population of university undergraduates in a Western country; whether the patterns of behaviour would generalize to other people was not known. The second wave of economic game findings led to more nuance; they revealed that how people behave in economic games depends. Macro studies revealed differences in average behaviour between different populations (Henrich et al., 2005; Herrmann et al., 2008), whilst micro studies revealed that small changes to the ways the games were set up led to quite different outcomes (Bardsley, 2007; Cronk & Wasielewski, 2008; Haley & Fessler, 2005). Economic games thus clearly had potential as assays of prosocial and antisocial motivations in our project, both for investigating neighbourhood differences and probing the decision-making processes that might underlie such differences. We ended up carrying out two different rounds of economic games, the first led by myself and Agathe Colléony, and the second by Kari Britt Schroeder. In each case, the questions we wanted to ask led us to develop new variant games, as well as new protocols for administering them that would allow people to play them with their neighbours and in their homes.

A major issue with economic games concerns their external validity. This has led to increasing discussion in the last few years (Bardsley, 2007; Burton-Chellew & West, 2013; Winking & Mizer, 2013). Do people really understand exactly what the contingencies of the game are? Would they behave in the same way if they did not know they were taking part in an experiment? Does a person's behaviour within the game bear any relationship to how they behave in everyday life? Given that we were going to use multiple methods, we would have the possibility of relating patterns of game play to other social measures, both at the individual and neighbourhood level. Both correspondences and non-correspondences would be interesting.

Correlational and experimental approaches

Social science is traditionally a correlational business, though people are increasingly interested in the potential for doing experiments. Correlational research means that you measure the pre-existing variation in something, say income or neighbourhood deprivation, and you see how it relates to variation in something else, say health. The Tyneside Neighbourhoods

Project was basically a correlational study, with neighbourhood as the initial predictor variable, and a whole host of other variables as secondary or mediating predictors. As I hinted in chapter 1, though, one of the key potential advantages of working at the meso-scale is that it raises the possibility of doing at least some experimental work.

It is important to be clear what experimental means here. Economic games are sometimes described as experimental, but this is a misnomer, since there is not necessarily experimental manipulation of any independent variable. The most famous results showing different economic game results in different cultural groups, for example, are purely correlational. When I say experimental work, I mean randomly assigning participants to a treatment that might produce a difference in a measured outcome—what in medicine and public policy is called a randomised control trial. The experiment in this sense is science's blue-chip method for providing insights about causality rather than just association. We did make a little progress in developing experimental approaches of this kind. We carried out two large-scale experiments and a few smaller ones. The design of each of these experiments was quite complex, and will make sense only once I have presented the bulk of the correlational data. I will therefore say nothing more about these experimental studies until it is time to look at their results, in chapter 4, and in chapter 6.

Ethical considerations

All empirical research raises ethical considerations, and the Tyneside Neighbourhoods Project was particularly ethically challenging. There were really two clusters of ethical issues: the first concerned the ethics of participation, and the second, the ethics of representation. The ethics of participation encompasses questions about what it was like to take part in the research: could any of the things we asked people to do cause them distress or harm, lead them to regret their participation, or make them feel aggrieved? These were, by and large, the easier issues to address. All of our research was scrutinized and approved by the Faculty of Medical Sciences ethics committee at Newcastle University. For observational studies, we only observed people in public settings where they could reasonably expect their behaviour to be observable anyway, and we never made any attempt to identify individuals. We were ready to be completely open about what we were doing if challenged, which we never were. For other kinds of studies, participants gave their written informed consent to participate, were fully debriefed, and of course were represented anonymously in all of our data.

We aimed to not deceive people. For example, when gave a financial dilemma about how to divide £10 between self and an anonymous third party, the money was always real, and we really find an anonymous third party and give her whatever was due. We did admittedly flirt with the boundaries of deceit at times. Dropping your keys on purpose to see if someone will pick them up for you is a kind of misrepresentation. We satisfied ourselves that the interaction was fleeting and the burden very small. In Kari Britt Schroeder's experiment described in chapter 4, we wanted to manipulate the social information that people had about what their neighbours thought, but we did not want to do this by making up false information. We found a solution whereby we gave them real information from real neighbours, but manipulated *which* neighbours they saw the information from. This achieved our experimental requirements whilst stopping short of deceit, though it could rather fairly be described as being economical with the truth.

The issues of ethics of representation concern the possible negative consequences for participants and their communities of the way we portrayed them in our publications and presentations. If the issues around the ethics of participation were soluble, those around the ethics of representation were much more of a concern to me, and remain so. Rather than discussing these any further at this point, I will return to them at the end of chapter 7, once we have seen the data. It is partly a concern with the ethics of representation that has led me to anonymize Neighbourhoods A and B. Anyone prepared to do some digging would be able to work out more or less where they are, but their specific identities are not put in the centre of the spotlight.

In the interests of full disclosure I should also say something about funding. I began the project with no funding beyond the fact that Newcastle University pays my salary. Students and other helpers mainly gave their labour voluntarily or as part of their programme of study. North Tyneside Council provided benefits in kind in the conduct of the School Survey described below. At later points, we were able to draw on resources from Newcastle University's funding of Gillian Pepper's PhD, and especially from a fellowship grant from the US National Science Foundation to Kari Britt Schroeder. The funders played no role in decisions about what to do or how to publish the results.

Description of datasets

Subsequent chapters of the book are organized thematically; each chapter draws on several different datasets, and each dataset is referred to in several different chapters. In the remainder of this chapter, then, I briefly describe each of the main datasets that we produced (as mentioned, leaving aside for now the two experimental datasets to be discussed in chapters 4 and 6). I will not repeat information such as sample size and method of collection when presenting results in future chapters; to find such information, the reader should return to this section. The citations shown as footnotes to the headings introducing each dataset refer to the published sources where the methods for that dataset are fully described. The raw data are freely available via an Open Science Framework project (Nettle, 2015) that can be found at https://osf.io/ys7g6.[1]

Observational Dataset 1[2]

The first and largest dataset involved direct behavioural observation on the streets of each neighbourhood. It was gathered, by me, between April 19th and July 8th 2010. The idea was to record everything happening on the streets for one whole spring/summer day, 9am to 9pm. Clearly, it would be impossible and undesirable to get all of the data on a single day. Instead, I divided the day into 24 half-hour segments (9:00–9:30, 9:30–10:00, etc.). I then chose a time segment pseudo-randomly (i.e. starting neither at the beginning of the day and working forwards, nor at the end and working backwards), went to one neighbourhood and recorded for that time segment. The next weekday I went to the other neighbourhood and recorded at the same time. Sometimes a weekend intervened, but the median delay between observing a time segment in the first neighbourhood and in the second was one day, and the maximum was four days. The order of the two neighbourhoods was counter-balanced across time segments. This process continued until all time segments had been filled in. All five weekdays were represented at least three times in both neighbourhoods. The observation period was outside the school holidays.

---

1   An archived version of the dataset, preserving the data in the form it was at the time of publication, is available at http://dx.doi.org/10.17605/OSF.IO/W9Z2P

2   Nettle, Colléony, & Cockerill, 2011; Nettle, 2011a, 2011c.

The first ten minutes of each segment were spent walking a transect up one side of the main street and down the other, the starting end varying randomly. The remaining twenty minutes were spent taking a random walk around the residential streets. I wore an unobtrusive digital voice recorder to capture the data to be transcribed later. With practice I developed an efficient numerical code for doing this; there was not a single instance where I felt that anyone noticed my *sotto voce* muttering.

My focus was on people—what they were doing and what kind of social groups they were doing it in—though I did capture some other information. For each social group that came into my sight and was not inside a building, I recorded the number of men, women, children, and babies. I recorded whether any of the individuals were smoking, drinking an alcoholic drink, or running. Social groups were defined on the basis of interaction or common movement; this was rarely difficult. A person on their own was classified as a social group of one. Individuals re-encountered within the same time segment were not recorded again. I additionally noted instances of some miscellaneous categories: babies crying, open front doors, people with walking sticks or wheelchairs, the dropping of litter, police patrols, and things on fire. The transcribed dataset contained data on 4123 social groups in Neighbourhood A, and 3773 in Neighbourhood B. In terms of people-observations, this equated to 5884 in Neighbourhood A and 6757 in Neighbourhood B.

Observational Dataset 2[3]

Observational Dataset 2 was gathered by Jessica Hill with the assistance of Ruth Jobling in the summer of 2013. Rather than sampling every minute of the day as in Observational Dataset 1, they sampled the first 30 minutes of every hour between 9am and 6pm inclusive (that is, 9–9:30, 10–10:30, etc.). They were able to complete this in two weeks, on some occasions gathering the data from the two neighbourhoods simultaneously on the same day, on others completing the time segment in the second neighbourhood the day after the first. Again, their sampling occurred during weekdays outside the school holidays.

Jessica and Ruth largely used the same protocol as in Observational Dataset 1. They observed a total of 3665 people across the two neighbourhoods.

---

3   Hill, Jobling, et al., 2014.

Their innovation was to code 'new' interactions. A 'new' interaction was defined as when an individual or group engaged in conversation with another individual or group they had not previously been interacting with. This could be anything from a fleeting greeting to stopping in the street to talk to someone. Jessica was interested in social ties, and this behavioural measure would give us some insight into the extent to which people in each neighbourhood knew others nearby well enough to talk to them. I am not sure whether Jessica was aware of this at the time, but her focus on new interactions relates closely to a dataset in Young and Willmott (1957 p. 84) where a resident recorded how many people that she knew she bumped into on the streets of Bethnal Green as she went about her daily business. Young and Willmott too saw this as an index of the density of social ties in the neighbourhood beyond the household. The findings from Observational Dataset 2 will be discussed in chapter 3 in particular.

Street Ages Dataset[4]

As a result of gathering Observational Dataset 1, we became interested in knowing which adults were using the streets, and in particular how this related to their age. To investigate this, Rebecca Coyne (in July and August 2010) and later Agathe Colléony (in April 2011) walked transects through the main streets of each neighbourhood, recording the sex and estimating the age of every person they passed. Unlike Observational Datasets 1 and 2, the Street Ages Dataset was gathered during the school holidays. Rebecca and Agathe each made six visits to each neighbourhood, alternating neighbourhoods and balancing approximate times of day. Rebecca coded for 15 minutes each time and Agathe for 30 minutes, giving a combined sample size of 2533 age-ratings. There were no significant differences in the distributions of ages in Rebecca and Agathe's data, and they were pooled for analysis.

Rebecca and Agathe's data only tell us about their *judgements* of age; we do not know the actual ages of the people that they saw. Previous research has indicated that visual judgements of age are fairly accurate (George & Hole, 1995). We knew from the 2001 census data what the 'true' distribution of chronological ages had looked like just a few years earlier, and so the null hypothesis was that their judged distribution of ages would be the same. Any systematic departure from the census distribution in one or both

---

4   Nettle, Coyne, & Colléony, 2012.

neighbourhoods would be telling. It might suggest neighbourhood-specific biases among those who, of all the people living there, used the streets.

Social Survey 1[5]

Social Survey 1 was the first major self-report assay we used in Neighbourhoods A and B. It also provided the vehicle for the first economic game, which will be described below. Its focus was on social relationships and prosocial behaviour. Social Survey 1 was largely implemented by Agathe Colléony. During the spring of 2011, we chose names and addresses in each neighbourhood from the electoral register, and sent a survey with a cover letter asking the addressed recipient if they would be so kind as to fill the survey out. A stamped return envelope was enclosed, and the respondent would also receive £10 for their trouble. 124 people returned surveys; 74 from Neighbourhood A and 50 from Neighbourhood B. This was after we had boosted the sampling in Neighbourhood B, since return rates were only 21.7% in Neighbourhood B as compared to 43.5% in Neighbourhood A.

The survey contained a number of demographic and attitudinal questions. Central to it was a measure of neighbourhood social capital. The concept of social capital is used somewhat variably in the literature (Halpern, 2005). Originally, it referred to resources that are embedded in the individual's social network; that is, having other people who know you, are well disposed to you, and are able to help you get things done. It is often used rather more loosely to denote positive feelings about social relationships or high trust within some group.

Our six key items to measure neighbourhood social capital included four questions on 7-point ratings scales: how much did the respondent trust other people in the neighbourhood, how much did they feel people in the neighbourhood looked out for one another, how well did they know their neighbours, and to what extent did they feel they had good friends living locally. The remaining two items were crude social network measures. First, we asked respondents to list all of the people they had contacted for social reasons within the last two weeks. They could use anonymizing initials for this, since we weren't interested in the names, but rather in how many of them there were. Second, we asked respondents to list all the people they could turn to if they had a problem. Human social networks are hierarchically

---

5   Nettle et al., 2011.

nested; every person is at the centre of several concentric circles, with the total number of people increasing as you move from the centre outwards, and emotional closeness and interaction intensity decreasing (Hill & Dunbar, 2003). Our two network measures were designed respectively to provide a rough measure of the size of the sympathy group, as the inner circle of frequently interacting friends and relatives is usually known, and the support clique, the smaller core of people one would rely on for the most serious needs. Previous studies have found that sympathy groups tend to number 10–12 individuals, and support cliques around 5 (Dunbar & Spoors, 1995). The means in our Social Survey 1 were correspondingly 11.65 and 6.23. Both measures had a right-skewed distribution, with some sympathy groups as large as 35 and support cliques as large as 32, but most much smaller. This is typical of previous studies. To a greater extent than some previous studies, we found women tended to have larger sympathy groups and support cliques than men (means for sympathy groups 13.90 vs. 9.01; for support cliques 6.84 vs. 5.16). Our six social capital items were rather heterogeneous in meaning, but, usefully, they were all substantially correlated with one another. This allowed us to combine them into a single index of social capital. The index had a Cronbach's α statistic of 0.81, which means that all six items correlated well with each other. Higher scores on this index equate to having a larger sympathy group and support clique, and to giving higher ratings of trust, indicating that people look out for each other, that the respondent knows neighbours, and that she has good friends living locally.

The first economic game was an integral part of Social Survey 1, but we did not want to draw attention to it as a measure of the study. This was because of the concerns that have been repeatedly raised about the effects of knowing that one is participating in a cooperation experiment on economic game behaviour (Bardsley, 2007). We therefore made our game relatively surreptitious. The respondent was told at the end of the questionnaire that she had finished and had earned £10 as a thank-you. A separate payment form then asked the respondent to provide the name and address to which she would like the money delivered. However, it also gave her the option of transferring some or all of the £10 to someone else rather than receiving it herself. This was in effect a version of the Dictator Game, the well-studied economic game in which an actor decides how a sum of money should be divided between himself and another individual, with that other individual having no say in the matter and no comeback. The Dictator Game is the simplest possible index of prosocial motivation:

how much money will you keep for yourself, and how much will you transfer to the other party? We will return to exactly what the versions of the Dictator Game we used were, and the motivation for them, in chapter 3. Once payment forms were received in the post, we hand-delivered the money, in cash, to the relevant addresses within one week.

Social Survey 2[6]

Social Survey 2 was envisaged and designed by Kari Britt Schroeder. She implemented it with assistance from Gillian Pepper and, to a much lesser extent, myself during 2012 and early 2013. Again, names and addresses were randomly chosen from the electoral register and the survey was delivered by mail with a return envelope. Care was taken not to resample individuals from Social Survey 1 and (for reasons to do with the associated economic game) not to choose immediate neighbours. It proved challenging to get a sufficient sample in Neighbourhood B given the constraints, and we extended the boundary of Neighbourhood B a few streets beyond its original limit. The extension area was similar to the original area on the relevant measures, such as the Index of Multiple Deprivation. The final sample size was 260, well balanced across the two neighbourhoods (A: 133; B: 127). Another 168 participants took part in an experimental add-on, to be described in chapter 4.

Whereas the focus of Social Survey 1 was on positive social resources and prosociality, the focus of Social Survey 2 was on the negative side of social interactions: breaking rules and harming others. The survey asked about a number of things, again including trust. This time we distinguished between trusting people in general and trusting people you know well. This had the potential to differentiate parochial social resources ('there is a small group of people I know well on whom I can rely') from more generalized trust ('I know that when I need something, anyone will help me out'). These could pattern differently across the two neighbourhoods. In addition, Kari investigated perceived norms of social behaviour. We will examine in more detail exactly how she did this in chapter 4. Kari's particular interest in perceived norms was in how they would relate to decisions in the economic game associated with Social Survey 2, to which I now turn.

---

6   Schroeder, Pepper, & Nettle, 2014.

The economic game associated with Social Survey 2 was a lot more complex than a Dictator Game. It thus could not be surreptitious, and a substantial fraction of the survey consisted of the questions involved in it. Given the focus on antisocial behaviour and its determinants, the game allowed some people the opportunity to behave antisocially, and others to the opportunity to administer justice by punishing that antisocial behaviour if they wished. The game had three roles, which will be explained in chapter 4. One third of the surveys sent out assigned their readers the role of player 1, the next third that of player 2, and the rest player 3. Specific triads were formed at random from surveys returned at around the same time from each neighbourhood; no respondent knew who the other members of their triad were. As before, all monies arising were delivered in cash to the respondents' addresses within one week.

Police Crime Dataset[7]

As we were interested in the topic of crime and antisocial behaviour, Agathe obtained data on all incidents reported to Northumbria Police between December 2010 and March 2011 falling within the study neighbourhoods (this information can be freely found via www.police.uk). As well as tabulating the number of incidents overall, she was able to break them down into different categories of crime or antisocial behaviour, as we will see in chapter 4.

Assorted assays of prosociality[8]

During 2011, we also undertook a number of other field assays of prosocial behaviour. The first of these used the lost letter paradigm, a classical unobtrusive measure of passer-by willingness to do an anonymous kindness. A stamped, addressed letter is left on the pavement in the general vicinity of a postal box. The measure is simply the proportion of letters that ever find their way to their recipient. The probability of return has been shown to vary, and to depend on a number of micro factors, such as the implied characteristics of the recipient, as well as macro factors, such as the community where the letter is left (Levine, Martinez, Brase, &

---

7   Nettle et al., 2011.
8   Nettle et al., 2011.

Sorenson, 1994; Milgram, Mann, & Harter, 1965). We left 22 letters in each neighbourhood on rain-free mornings over the course of several months.

In addition to the lost letter, we employed three other helping assays from classic social psychological literature (Levine et al., 1994): dropped object, asking directions, and making change. In dropped object, 24 volunteer field assistants walked along the street and, seemingly inadvertently, dropped a small object such as keys, a glove or a pen around 10m in front of a pedestrian approaching in the other direction. We scored whether or not the target person helped by drawing attention to or picking up the object. The same volunteer field assistant then dropped the same object in the other neighbourhood. There were a total of 60 drops in each neighbourhood. Characteristics of both dropper and target, such as age and sex, were recorded. Asking directions and making change were very similar paradigms, except that the volunteer field assistants (the same ones as for dropped object) asked either for directions to a nearby hospital (there was a suitable one close to both neighbourhoods) or to make change from a large-denomination coin. Trials were scored as minimal or no help versus substantial help. There were 30 trials in each neighbourhood for each assay.

Field assays of social behavioural such as these have been extensively used in the past. Lost letter and making change are becoming obsolete due to changes in technology (what do you need a 10p coin for anymore?). Even asking for directions seems a little unnatural when most young people carry smartphones. Nonetheless, we were able to obtain datasets using all of these, and they will be discussed in chapter 3.

School Survey[9]

The final dataset is the only one that was not gathered in Neighbourhoods A and B, and also the only one where we heard from young people. In 2009, Maria Cockerill and I surveyed 1046 school students aged 9–15 from various parts of Tyneside other than Neighbourhoods A and B. They were from eight different schools, and their residential addresses could be assigned to eight different neighbourhoods, for each of which we obtained an Index of Multiple Deprivation. The School Survey proved useful in a number of ways. It provided some data from very deprived neighbourhoods of Tyneside other than Neighbourhood B (along the Eastern riverside); it provided some

---

9   Nettle & Cockerill, 2010.

data from an affluent area of Tyneside other than Neighbourhood A (in the East of the conurbation); and it provided data from some intermediate neighbourhoods too, rather than just having the two extremes as in Social Surveys 1 and 2. Thus, it helped to generalize beyond the main two study neighbourhoods and across the spectrum of deprivation. Moreover, by surveying children at different ages, we could get some ideas about how the characteristic attitudes and feelings of deprived neighbourhoods develop through childhood. I say some ideas rather than any stronger inference, because this was not a truly longitudinal study; rather, we surveyed cross-sections of Tyneside children at several different ages. Nonetheless, it did allow us to identify which patterns were apparent in which age groups.

The School Survey was a comprehensive questionnaire whose original aims were to do with the psychological consequences of deprivation and the factors related to early childbearing. It contained questions about the respondents' ideal age of parenthood and anticipated life expectancy. It also contained measures of the neighbourhood's perceived safety and the respondent's perceived support from their family. Finally, it asked about trust, linking it the social capital work in Social Surveys 1 and 2.

I have now described all of the main datasets that made up the Tyneside Neighbourhoods Project. With this preliminary work done, we can turn to the substantive findings. These are laid out in chapters 3–6. Chapters 3 and 4 respectively examine prosocial and antisocial behaviour amongst adults. Chapter 5 explores how neighbourhood differences vary with age. Chapter 6 focuses on questions of psychological mechanism, asking how variation in experience might lead to variation in attitudes and hence to variation in social behaviour. Chapter 7 concludes with my overall reflections on what we learned.

3. Mutual aid

Don't push me 'cos I'm close to the edge;
I'm trying not to lose my head...

Introduction

This chapter deals with prosocial behaviour; that is, behaviour that helps someone else. The beneficiary can be specific, as when one aids a friend in need, or more diffuse, as when one cleans up the street, benefitting anyone who happens to use it. The behaviour is prosocial in either case. Note that a behaviour being prosocial does not mean self-interest must be absent. Many of the things people do together involve both parties benefitting, and these would still be classed as prosocial. Even where one party does not obviously benefit in the short term, she may in the longer run. For example, donating money to a community organization appears on the face of it to be completely altruistic, but the donor may obtain long-term favours or reputational benefits by doing so. We will not be concerned here with whether prosocial behaviour can always be shown to be a form of enlightened self-interest, but rather with whether and why patterns of prosocial behaviour differ across the two neighbourhoods.

There are many kinds of prosocial interactions woven into the life of any community. Indeed, community is sometimes defined in terms of social interactions beyond the scope of the household but short of the scope of formal or governmental institutions. Prosocial interactions beyond the household relate closely to the notion of social capital: resources and investments embedded or distributed in a social network. You may recall from chapter 1 that we have two broad and opposing narratives about deprivation and prosociality available to us. The Kropotkinian narrative leads us to expect greater prosociality in Neighbourhood B, and the Mountain People narrative leads us to expect greater prosociality in Neighbourhood A. The bulk of this chapter is devoted to examining our various datasets in the light of these opposing sets of expectations.

  http://dx.doi.org/10.11647/OBP.0084.03

Round one: Social interactions in the streets

We should be able to learn a lot about people's social behaviours by seeing how they associate on the streets. First, then, let us examine the patterns in Observational Dataset 1. The simplest question we can ask is: how many people are on the street? The upper plots of Figure 3.1 show the data by time of day, separately for the main and residential streets. As you can see, the two main streets follow roughly the same pattern across the day, though main street A is busier than B: people come out into the main street during commercial hours to do what they need to do in the shops and banks; by evening, the main streets have become empty of people. The more interesting difference is in the residential streets. In Neighbourhood A, there is a steady flow of pedestrians in the residential streets through the day, but after 17:00, it drops off precipitately. People have gone into their houses. In Neighbourhood B by contrast, they continued to be outside their houses in considerable numbers until I stopped recording data at 21:00. In fact, the residential streets of Neighbourhood B are busier in the evening than at any point during the day.

Part of the relative excess of people on the residential streets of B in the evening is attributable to the greater prevalence of children 'playing out', a phenomenon to which we return in chapter 5. But the focus of this chapter is on adult social behaviour, so let us ignore children for now. The lower panels of Figure 3.1 plot the same data, but for adults only. We see a similar pattern; after around 18:00, there are essentially no adults on the residential streets of A, whereas they continue to be on the residential streets of B in considerable numbers until the end of recording at 21:00. (Recall that these data were gathered in the summer when dusk is considerably later than 21:00.)

Not only are the adults in Neighbourhood A inside their houses in the evening; they have closed their doors. Figure 3.2 plots the number of front doors open by time of day in the residential streets of each neighbourhood. As is clear, the residents of B, as well as being more likely to be outside, are much more likely to have their front doors open. The meaning of this is hard to determine; their houses are smaller on average, for one thing. However, the door being open at least allows for the possibility of social interaction, and it does suggest that people are not secluding themselves, embattled, from the danger of encounter with their neighbours. I have had occasion to wander into houses with open doors in Neighbourhood B, in search of someone to give money to, including on occasions when the resident turned out to be elsewhere despite the door being open.

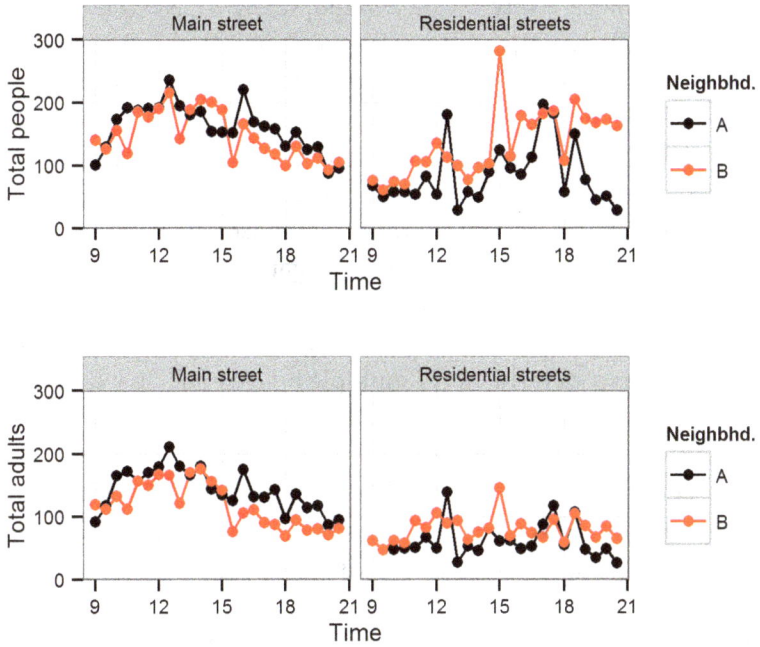

Figure 3.1 Total numbers of people (upper plots) and adults (lower plots) by time of day and neighbourhood in Observational Dataset 1. Image © Daniel Nettle, CC BY.

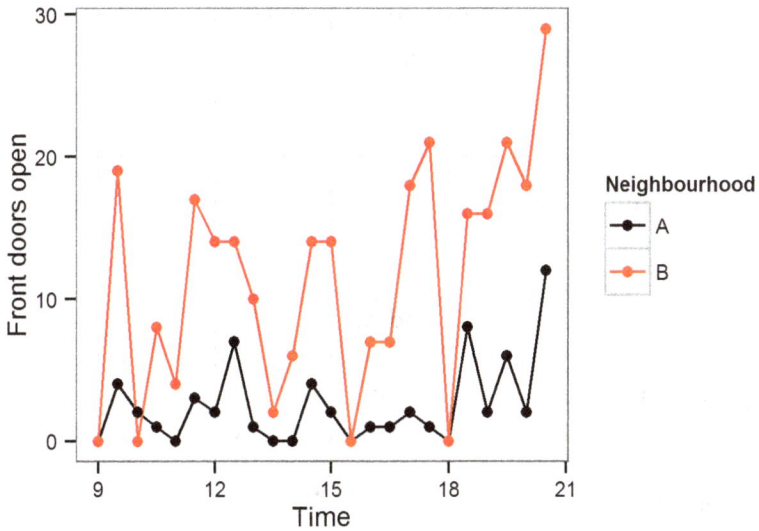

Figure 3.2 The number of open front doors by time of day and neighbourhood in Observational Dataset 1. Image © Daniel Nettle, CC BY.

So adults are more likely to be on the street in Neighbourhood B, especially in the evenings. What are they doing there? One thing they are doing that you do not see in Neighbourhood A is street drinking. The rising cost of drinking in pubs, coupled with people's relatively straitened means, has largely destroyed that traditional working-class institution in Neighbourhood B. However, alcoholic beverages are inexpensive in shops, where they are bought for off-the-premises consumption. People consume beer in particular in impromptu gatherings in gardens, parks, and street corners. It is not uncommon to see sofas and dining chairs dragged outside to facilitate these gatherings, and it is my impression that they typically involve residents of multiple households. In Observational Dataset 1, I observed 38 instances of street drinking in Neighbourhood B as against 1 in Neighbourhood A; these involved a mean of 3.21 people (standard deviation 1.89). Most people on the residential streets of Neighbourhood B were not involved in street drinking. Nonetheless, there was plenty of social interaction going on, as the street drinking parties demonstrate.

These evening gatherings exemplify a more general pattern in Observational Dataset 1: adults are less likely to be alone in Neighbourhood B than A. Figure 3.3 shows the mean number of adults in a social group by time of day and neighbourhood. Groups consisting wholly of children are excluded. As you can see, the mean is fairly close to 1 at all times. Adults are always moderately likely to be alone (or at least, the lone adult) as they go about their neighbourhoods. However, there is a clear neighbourhood difference; adult group sizes are consistently larger in Neighbourhood B, and this is driven by adults in B, at all times of day, being rather more likely to be with another adult.

It is very unlikely that this pattern simply reflects adults going outside with the people they live with. As you may recall from chapter 2, in Neighbourhood B, there are many more households headed by a lone adult than is true in Neighbourhood A. Thus, if people go out of the house with the people they live with, we should expect to see smaller adult group sizes in B than A. The fact that we observed exactly the opposite suggests strongly that adults in B are more heavily involved than those in A in day-to-day social interaction with other local adults who are not members of their households.

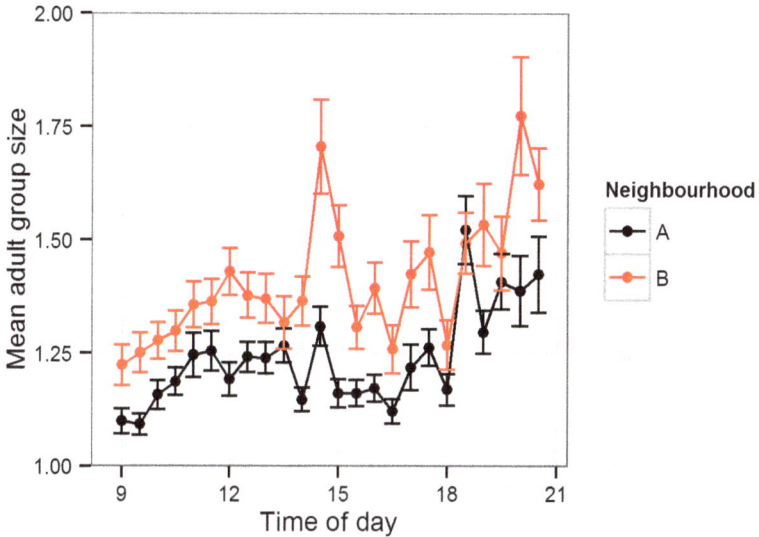

Figure 3.3 Mean number of adults in each social group by neighbourhood and time of day in Observational Dataset 1. Groups consisting solely of children are excluded. Error bars represent one standard error. Image © Daniel Nettle, CC BY.

We can drill down further into what kinds of associations are driving the differences. Figure 3.4 shows the relative prevalence of men alone, women alone, male-female couples, and other types of group across the two neighbourhoods in Observational Dataset 1. The other groups of interest are multi-male groups (several men but no women), multi-female groups (several women but no men), and mixed groups (more than two adults, both sexes present). As the figure shows, adults of both sexes are less likely to be on their own in Neighbourhood B, though the neighbourhood difference is much stronger for women than men. The reduction in aloneness is made up for by a relative increase in same-sex associations for both sexes, and also in more mixed-sex groups of more than two, in Neighbourhood B. Only some of this is driven by the street drinking groups. There are also, for example, many more groups consisting of several females and their young children out and about in Neighbourhood B (93 such groups observed in B against 21 in A). Male-female couples are about equally prevalent in the two neighbourhoods, though this in itself is something of a surprise, since there are many more lone-female-headed households in Neighbourhood B than A. We might thus have expected fewer opposite-sex couples on the street, but this is not so.

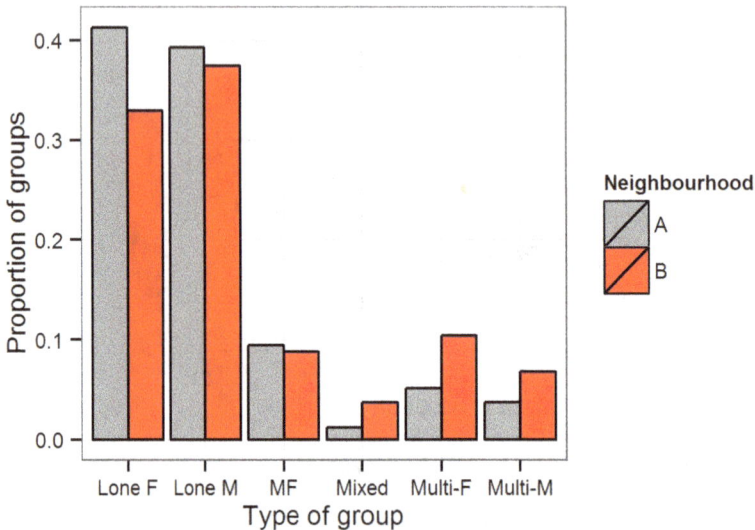

Figure 3.4 The proportions of adult social groups that are of various compositions by neighbourhood in Observational Dataset 1. Image © Daniel Nettle, CC BY.

Observational Dataset 2 provided similar information to Observational Dataset 1, albeit gathered three years later. Jessica and Ruth confirmed many of the same patterns I had seen (see Hill, Jobling, et al., 2014 for a detailed analysis). Adult group sizes were significantly larger in B than A. This was again driven by adults of both sexes being significantly less likely to be on their own. Indeed, in Observational Dataset 2, the odds of an adult being with another adult were twice as high in B than A. The novel addition of Observational Dataset 2 was Jessica and Ruth's examination of 'new' social interactions. To recall, these were defined as instances when an individual or group in the street engaged in conversation with another individual or group they had not previously been interacting or moving with. 'New' interactions give us a metric of how often someone in the neighbourhood bumps into someone else they know well enough to want to say hello. Jessica and Ruth observed 62 'new' interactions in A and 120 in B during their period of sampling. Correcting for the different total numbers of people observed, the odds of an adult engaging in a 'new' interaction in

B were 2.3 times higher than in A. The difference was particularly marked in the early evening (as we approach the time of street socializing in B), when they saw 37 'new' interactions in B and just 6 in A (Figure 3.5).

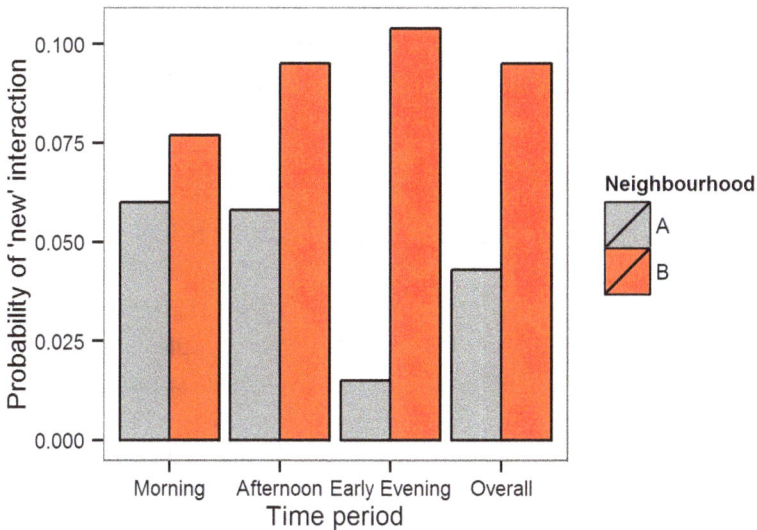

Figure 3.5 The probability an observed adult engages in a 'new' interaction, by neighbourhood and time period of the day, from Observational Dataset 2. Image © Daniel Nettle, CC BY.

The patterns in Observational Datasets 1 and 2 bring to mind Kropotkin — and Young and Willmott's (1957) depiction of working-class Bethnal Green — much more than they bring to mind the Mountain People narrative. In the deprived Neighbourhood B, it seems, adults seek out other adults and interact socially with them. They are more likely to go around the neighbourhood with someone else, especially in the case of women; their front doors are more likely to be open; there are more informal social gatherings on the street; and they stop and greet each other more as they move around. We do not know what social interactions are going on inside the houses in either neighbourhood, or being transacted via phones and email. This is a big limitation. However, the difference in life on the streets is fairly marked, and it would not be totally unreasonable to assume that it is roughly representative of the difference in social interactions of other kinds too. We have no sense from the observational findings of what the *quality* of social relationships is, or what kinds of prosocial services are provided through them. Nonetheless, it seems that Neighbourhood B is the more social place, where interaction between adults is much more pervasive.

Round two: Self-reported social capital

Social Survey 1 asked people six key questions about social networks and social capital (to recall, these concerned trust within the neighbourhood, knowing neighbours, having good friends living locally, people in the neighbourhood looking out for one another, social contacts, and support cliques). Given the results of the previous section, the clear expectation is that residents of B will report that they know their neighbours better and have more good friends living locally than residents of A. All those open doors and street greetings might mean than they trust their neighbours more in B than A, and feel more strongly that people look out for one another. When asked about social contacts and social support, residents of B might well produce a greater number of contacts than those of A, though this prediction is less clear than the previous ones, because these last two survey questions do not exclusively concern social interactions within the neighbourhood. Residents of A might have large social networks and engage in extensive social interaction, just geographically elsewhere. Nonetheless, the result that would be most consilient with the observational data, as well as easiest to make sense of in a Kropotkinian kind of way, would be higher social capital in B than A by all measures.

The results are exactly the opposite. There are substantial neighbourhood differences on all the social capital measures, but social capital is in all cases higher in A than B (Figure 3.6). If we take the right-hand two pairs of bars in Figure 3.6 first, we see that respondents from B have smaller numbers of people in their sympathy groups and support cliques than respondents from A. There is no necessary contradiction between this and the results we have already seen showing more spontaneous social interaction in B. Perhaps people in B concentrate on fewer, deeper relationships, whilst people in A have more numerous but less intense social contacts. The first four pairs of bars, though, present a paradox: although the observational data shows that there is demonstrably less interaction between neighbours in A, respondents there trust each other more, feel they know each other better, feel that they have better friends locally, and feel more strongly that people in their neighbourhood look out for one another.

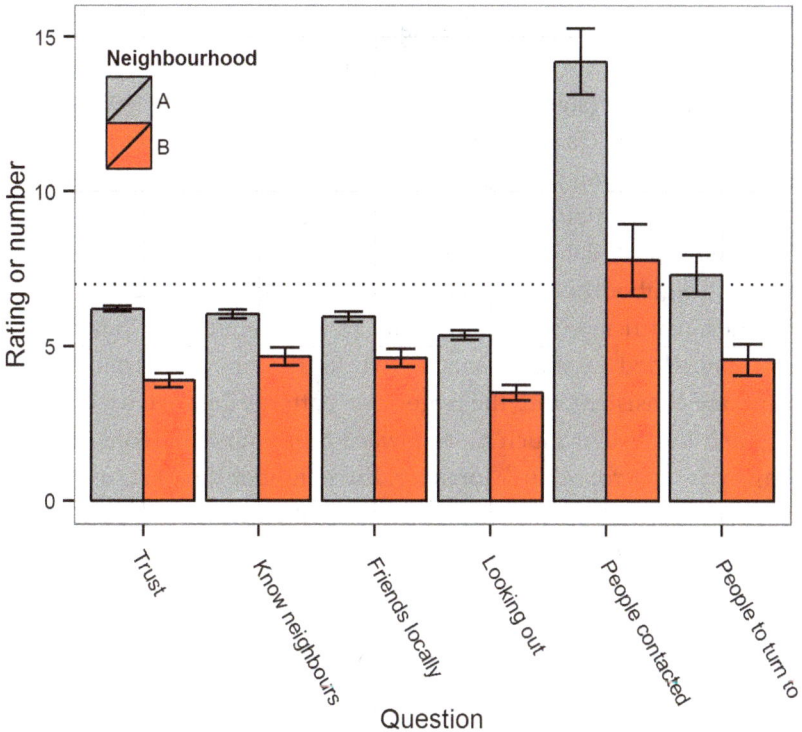

Figure 3.6 Means and standard errors for the six social capital measures in the Social Survey 1 dataset. The dotted horizontal line represents the maximum possible rating for the first four questions, which were scored on a 1–7 scale. The last two questions involved the respondent enumerating people they had contacted or could turn to. Image © Daniel Nettle, CC BY.

Before turning to the question of how to reconcile these findings with those from the direct observational data, we will just check that they are reproducible in other datasets. In Social Survey 2 (which, remember, was a different and larger set of respondents), Kari also had questions about trust. Trust is a key marker of social capital, and in Social Survey 1, the trust response was highly correlated with the responses to the other social capital questions. In Social Survey 2, Kari distinguished between social trust, which is trust of people you do not know well, and personal trust, which is trust of people you do know well. Both were measured on a 10–point scale.

The results were much the same as those from Social Survey 1, in that there was significantly lower trust in B than A. Interestingly, this applied to both types of trust. For social trust, the mean in A was 5.00 (standard deviation 1.86), compared to 3.53 (standard deviation 2.05) in B. For personal trust, the mean in A was 8.61 (standard deviation 1.24), compared to 7.97 (standard deviation 1.88) in B. Thus, in Neighbourhood B, the pattern of relatively low trust encompassed not just strangers, but also people the respondent knew well. This is a potentially important observation, to which I will return.

The self-report data, then, all point in the same direction. In the deprived Neighbourhood B, people trust each other less, feel they know each other insufficiently, and generally report feeling that they have *less* capital embedded in their social networks than people from A. These findings are consistent with the large-scale patterns detected by Haushofer (2013), and they point much more toward the Mountain People narrative and away from Kropotkin. Moreover, the neighbourhood differences are large. One way to illustrate this is to compare the data from Social Survey 1 to the World Values Survey data from other populations. The World Values Survey uses its questions about trust to compute a country-level trust index; this index is on a scale where 0 represents total distrust, 200 total trust, and 100 an equal balance of trust and distrust. With a little kneading, I can use our data to produce the same index for Neighbourhoods A and B as if they too were countries.

Figure 3.7 compares Neighbourhoods A and B to a selection of World Values Survey countries. Neighbourhood A scores a little less than 100. This puts it somewhat below the remarkably trusting Scandinavian countries, but slightly above many of the major industrial economies such as Germany and the USA. Its score is very similar to Canada's. Neighbourhood B, by contrast, scores about 28. This puts it in the company of populations in the developing world; ahead of Kenya, about equal to Zimbabwe, but some distance below Burkina Faso and Colombia. This seems like a difference big enough to concern us—a difference that is socially and not just statistically significant.

So far, we have one set of measures lining up on the side of each of our two narratives: direct behavioural observation for Kropotkin and self-report surveys for the Mountain People. Perhaps the third type of measure, economic games, will help adjudicate between them.

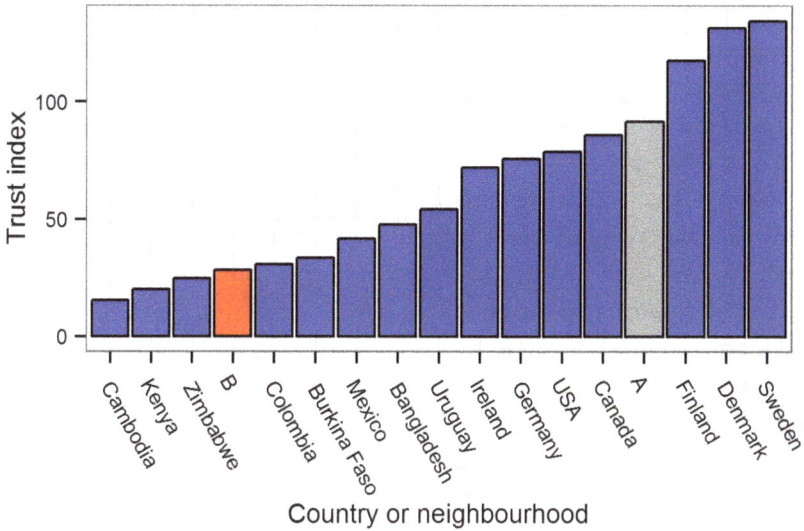

Figure 3.7 World Values Survey Trust Index for a number of countries, and for Neighbourhoods A and B. Country data is from http://www.jdsurvey.net/jds/jdsurvey Maps.jsp?Idioma=I&SeccionTexto=0404&NOID=104 (January 2015), and indices for A and B have been constructed using data from Social Survey 1. Image © Daniel Nettle, CC BY.

Round three: Dictator Games

The economic games for studying prosociality that we implemented in Neighbourhoods A and B were attached to Social Survey 1. The respondents had been told that they would be recompensed £10 for their trouble. At the end of the survey, they found a form asking them to specify how that £10 would be given out. They could choose some amount to be delivered in cash to their own address, with the remainder to be delivered to someone else (see below on exactly who the someone else was). We were thus implementing a version of the Dictator Game. Because of concerns about demand characteristics (people making particular decisions because they know they are taking part in a study of prosociality for which the researcher has certain expectations), we tried to make our game surreptitious. That is, the participants were not told that this decision about the disposition of the £10 payment was itself part of the study. We do not know the extent to which they figured out that it was, and whether this differed between neighbourhoods.

The Dictator Game is perhaps best thought of as a measure of the participant's motivation to make a social investment with a monetary resource, rather than keeping it for private use. In general terms, then, we could make predictions about neighbourhood differences either way. The Kropotkinian view, the direct behavioural observation results, and previous studies on socioeconomic variation in generosity (Piff et al., 2010) clearly suggest that transfers to the other party would be higher in B than A. The Mountain People hypothesis, and the data on social capital and trust, points firmly in the opposite direction.

In fact, we implemented three subtly different versions of the Dictator Game, each with a separate group of participants. In the first version, the *standard condition*, the instructions allowed the respondent to specify an amount in pounds, including zero, to be delivered to a randomly-chosen name and address in their neighbourhood. The balance would be delivered to the respondent's own house. We stressed that the respondent would remain anonymous whatever decision she made, and that she would also not know the identity of any beneficiary. Thus, this situation equates fairly closely to a laboratory Dictator Game as usually performed.

In the second version, the *friend condition*, we allowed the respondent to nominate the recipient, with the condition that the person must be someone in the neighbourhood. In addition, we explained that we would double any amount transferred. The motivation for this non-standard version of the Dictator Game was the hypothesis that people in Neighbourhood B might be less inclined to help someone in general, but more inclined to make a social investment in a particular individual they were close to (that is, their cooperation might be more parochial, centred on people they knew well). Allowing the respondent to nominate the recipient had the potential to reveal the existence of close prosocial ties within the neighbourhood. Moreover, the doubling of the stake made cooperation relatively attractive: the respondent could nominate a friend over the road and transfer £10, which would be turned into £20. The two could then meet up and split the money evenly and the respondent would have lost nothing. This would work fine as long as he or she had a trusted partner suitable for the endeavour living nearby. We predicted we might see greater transfers in Neighbourhood B than Neighbourhood A in this second condition, even if no differences (or the opposite difference) could be seen in the first, standard condition Dictator Game.

In the final version, the *charity condition*, any money transferred would again be doubled, but the recipient a locally-based charity (specified by us) that was well-known in both neighbourhoods. Thus, this condition featured doubling like the second condition, but without the respondent being able to choose the recipient.

The results are shown in Figure 3.8. In Neighbourhood A, the results for the standard and friend conditions are much the same as those observed in many studies of developed Western populations; many but not all people transfer something, and the mean transfer is of the order of 40–50% of the stake. (Rather surprisingly, transfers were no higher in the friend than the standard condition.) The charity condition produced greater generosity still.

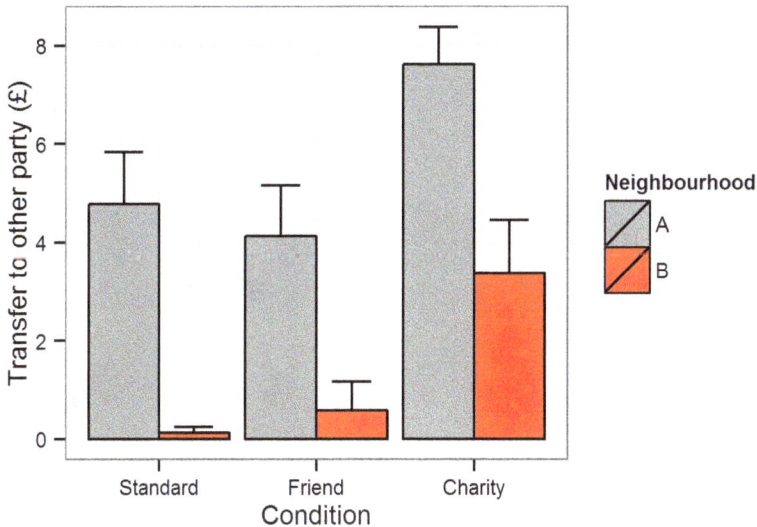

Figure 3.8 Mean transfers in the three conditions of the Dictator Game across the two neighbourhoods. Error bars represent one standard error. Image © Daniel Nettle, CC BY.

Neighbourhood B looked quite different; transfers were dramatically lower across the board. In fact, in Neighbourhood B, almost nobody transferred anything in the standard or friend conditions (2 people out of 33, against 21 out of 45 for Neighbourhood A). The results were particularly striking for two reasons. The first is that (to our disappointment) it did not matter which version of the Dictator Game we looked at; the neighbourhood difference was always in the same direction. People in B were just less likely to make transfers regardless of which condition they were in. Second, the differences were large. To put them into context, a famous cross-cultural study including societies on different continents and at radically different stages in economic development showed what they characterized as dramatic variation in, *inter alia*, Dictator Game behaviour (Henrich et al., 2010). We can overlay the results from our standard condition on theirs (Figure 3.9). As you can see, the difference we observed across neighbourhoods within this single city was much more dramatic than the largest they documented by comparing people from rural Missouri and from small-scale societies in Papua New Guinea or East Africa.

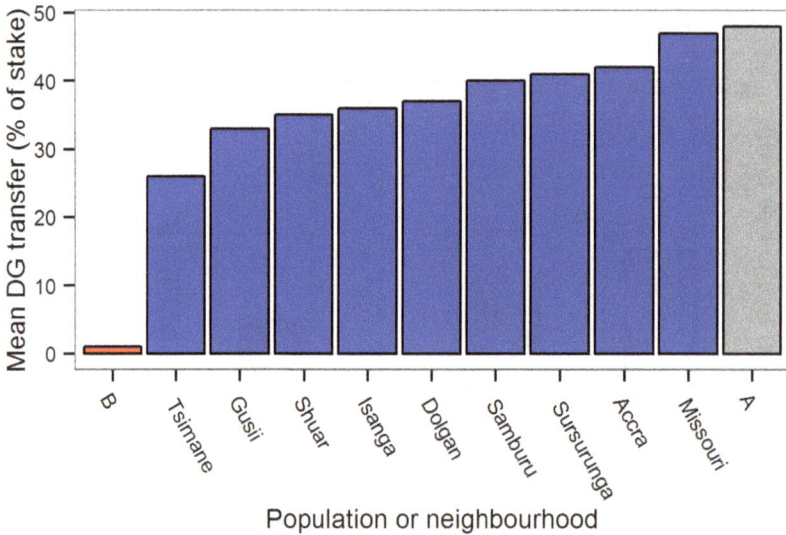

Figure 3.9 Mean Dictator Game transfer for the two study neighbourhoods and ten societies from Henrich et al.'s (2010) cross-cultural study. Image © Daniel Nettle, CC BY.

There are some important technical differences between the studies. Henrich et al. (2010) adjusted the stake to local resource values. We did not do this and, ideally, the stake would have been larger in A than B to make its relative value more comparable. However, the general consensus in the behavioural economic literature is that decisions in games such as these are relatively impervious to variation in the size of the stake (Carpenter, Verhoogen, & Burks, 2005; Forsythe, Horowitz, Savin, & Sefton, 1994). On the other hand, in many ways, our study was much better controlled than that of Henrich et al. (2010), since we were able to deliver exactly the same instructions, in the same language and the same way, in our two sites. Thus, the magnitude of the difference does seem noteworthy, and its direction decidedly unfavourable to Kropotkin and reminiscent of the Mountain People.

The neighbourhood difference in Dictator Game transfers was tightly bound up with the neighbourhood difference in self-reported social capital. That is, people in B tend to have lower social capital than those in A; people with lower social capital transferred less in the Dictator Game; and this explains a sizable portion of the neighbourhood difference in Dictator Game transfers. It makes sense that people with lower social capital would transfer less. Presumably we are willing to invest resources in our social network to the extent that we feel we have a potentially fruitful social network to invest in; the poorer we feel it is, the more we will want to keep our resources to ourselves.

Close to the edge

This section is devoted to trying to make some theoretical sense of the data presented so far. Behavioural observation shows people interacting more in the streets, socializing more, being alone less often, showing signs of knowing one another, and having their front doors open more in Neighbourhood B than A. On the other hand, people in Neighbourhood B say they *feel* that they don't know their neighbours as well, they don't trust them as much, and they don't feel they have such supportive social networks. Moreover, when you give them, through the Dictator Game, a chance to make a social investment, they are much less keen to do it, even when they can choose the beneficiary. How can we make sense of this pattern?

I am going to assume that each type of measure has some value. That is, I am not going to dismiss one kind of measure (e.g. self-report) as just less reliable than another (e.g. direct observation), and therefore claim that one gives us the 'true' picture and the other, junk. Rather, I will assume that all kinds of measures are giving us real information about something, but that something might not be the same in each case. A corollary of this is that both of the Kropotkin and Mountain People narratives are probably capturing something about real life.

To make sense of the data, I would like to build on a number of propositions, some of which I can evidence later and some of which I cannot, though they are plausible. The first of these is that people in Neighbourhood B tend to be, in a sense I will explain shortly, closer to the edge than those in Neighbourhood A. What do I mean by close to the edge? There are various domains of life where, as things get increasingly unfavourable, it becomes worthwhile to do things that would, the rest of the time, be extremely unwise. This prediction is set out with particular clarity in so-called risk-sensitive foraging models in animal behaviour (Stephens, 1981). An animal with sufficient energy reserves should prefer a food patch that provides a small sure yield over one that sometimes provides a bonanza and often provides nothing. However, when that animal's reserves get so low that it is close to the edge of starvation, only a bonanza would be enough to get it back up to safety. It should thus go to the often-bad-but-occasional-bonanza patch; it will probably get nothing and starve, but it is so close to the edge that it will certainly starve anyway if it goes to the safe patch. So, a gamble that might normally be a really bad idea becomes attractive when you are close to the edge. Importantly for our purposes, the models suggest that there is a point close to the edge of starvation where the individual's behaviour should flip, from strongly preferring the safe option to strongly preferring the gamble. (The theoretical predictions from risk-sensitive foraging models are clear. However, it is not clear that animals' behaviour actually conforms to these predictions, though people have tried hard to find evidence that they do [Kacelnik & Bateson, 1996; Kacelnik & El Mouden, 2013]. That however is a story for another day.)

We can generalize the idea of people's behaviour flipping when they are close to the edge (Nettle, 2009). It is not just starvation that might cause such a flip, but financial crisis or any other form of existential threat. For example, it is normally a really bad idea to take things from your neighbours, as they will probably provide you with more benefits over the long run through friendship than the short-term resource you might get away with (and, needless to say, you will lose their friendship if you take things from them). However, as you get close to the edge of financial crisis, you begin to need money just to get to the end of the week. You no longer have the luxury of considering the benefits that might accrue over many years; you will not be able to *have* many years unless you can overcome your immediate shortfall. So, your behaviour might flip and you might do something impulsive like robbing your neighbours. We can think of many domains where this principle might apply: financial risk-taking, betraying friendships, breaking social norms and rules, using coercion or deceit. As you get close to the edge, there may come a point where you suddenly start to have a reason for doing these things.

I am not saying that deprivation provides uniformly greater incentives for committing desperate or risky acts. If limited finances mean that you can't get yourself out of trouble or move away to another town, then it might be all the more important, most of the time, *not* to be deceitful, selfish, or risk-prone. However, deprivation might move people into a space where they are hovering so close to an edge that they oscillate stochastically between a state of necessary prudence and a state where they feel they have to do desperate things urgently just to get through their immediate crisis. This is the edge principle: if you live your life close the edge, your behaviour is likely to be more variable than if you live your life far from the edge.

Let us see how this might work. In a very deprived context, most people most of the time are hard at work just getting by and have to be very careful in doing so, since their means are limited and prospects uncertain. However, life shocks (financial, health, personal) are constantly happening. People far from the edge can absorb these shocks with no radical changes to their behaviour, since they have enough of a financial and emotional buffer to do so. For people already under great strain, a life shock might be enough to push them to the edge, and thus their behaviour will suddenly become very different from what it was last week. As if to illustrate this point, on June 26th 2014, the Newcastle *Evening Chronicle* reported the case of a pair of men who stormed into one of the bookmaker's shops on the main street of Neighbourhood B and threatened staff with metal bars, making off with several hundred pounds. They were instantly caught by police, and turned out to be locals. 'I can't believe I did it. I go in that bookies all the time', one of them commented, adding: 'I did it to pay for my dad's funeral'. Such striking temporal variability in behaviour would be unlikely to happen in a population where everyone was far from the edge to begin with.

The more variable something is, the more information you require to predict it and therefore make appropriate decisions about it (Frankenhuis & Panchanathan, 2011). If the people in your neighbourhood are—at least some of them, at least some of the time—close to the edge, then it makes sense that even if you had a lot of interaction with them, you might not feel that you had *enough* interaction to say you knew what they were going to do next. By contrast, if the people in your neighbourhood were always far from the edge, then even if you had only very limited and infrequent interaction with them, it might well be enough—enough to say you knew them, enough to feel you could turn to them, enough to trust them—simply because there was so little variability in their behaviour over time.

Now let us apply these principles to the interpretation of our data. First, as the behavioural observation suggests, it is likely that the residents of B do rely more on their neighbourhood social networks than the residents of A to accomplish the things they need. After all, they have less money on average and poorer access to the technologies and institutions that money and professional status can give access to. Yet at the same time as they possibly rely more on their social networks, the surveys show that they feel the inadequacy of these bonds all the more keenly. The stakes are probably higher in that they really need those bonds to work, yet the predictability of their social ties is lower because of the greater behavioural variability discussed above. The greater investment in informal socializing in Neighbourhood B might be considered an attempt to reduce uncertainty, by gathering more data on how other people are currently disposed. Even with this extra data, though, people's subjective experience is of greater mistrust and social anxiety; the extra data people have about the behaviour of others is not enough to outweigh the extra variability in that behaviour. This view makes a novel testable prediction: interpersonal relationships in Neighbourhood B should show greater temporal variability than those in A; at times people will be close, but they will also have occasional, dramatic fallings out. By contrast, relationships in A should show a flatter line over time. I haven't directly tested this hypothesis. In Observational Dataset 1, I coded the occurrence of clear altercations going on in the street. I saw 3 in Neighbourhood B and none in A. The numbers are too small to warrant much of a conclusion, especially given that people in A may choose to conduct their altercations in the privacy of their homes.

What I have said so far in this section appears sufficient to explain the gulf between behaviour and self-report. It also explains why trust would be lower in Neighbourhood B, even trust of people well-known to the respondent, since trust is to a very considerable extent a metric of our belief in the predictability of others' behaviour. How though can we explain the Dictator Game results? The Dictator Game is an assay of motivation to make an avoidable social investment. (It is avoidable since by transferring zero, in our implementation of the Dictator Game at any rate, you can avoid the need for any third party to become involved in the strange business at all.) The attractiveness of making an avoidable social investment will depend a lot on your perception of the predictability and reliability of the social actors with whom that investment would be made. If predictability and reliability are low, there is a risk inherent in the social investment that you do not run if you just keep all the money to yourself. This might explain the unwillingness of respondents in B to make transfers. It is not that their transfers were small, but rather that they did not want to get another person involved at all. Interestingly, in the charity condition, where the other party was not a person in the same neighbourhood, but a well-known and presumably reliable regional organization, the proportion of Neighbourhood B respondents making a transfer dramatically increased.

We may also have explained the diametric difference between our findings and those of Piff and colleagues (Piff et al., 2010). To recall, they found that people of lower socioeconomic position were relatively more generous using assays like the Dictator Game. However, they measured prosociality in general settings, not prosociality specifically directed towards other people who are experiencing deprivation. In most of their studies, the participants were individuals who had made it as far as university. This means that the participants' backgrounds were probably a lot less deprived than those of our Neighbourhood B participants. More importantly, it means that the *targets* of the participants' social investments were not people close to the edge. They were implied to be others from the university community. Thus, the participants in those studies were facing a very different social allocation decision compared to ours: whether to invest in a generally middle-class social group, regardless of their own social background. It is perhaps not surprising that those from humbler backgrounds wanted to invest more in that social group, but this is a different question from whether the residents of Neighbourhood B want to invest in the other residents of their neighbourhood.

The return of the lost letter, and other encounters

The conclusion of the foregoing section was that people in Neighbourhood B are more uncertain about what others in their neighbourhood will do, which makes them feel anxious and negative about social relationships even in the face of abundant interaction. It also means that if they have a choice between opening up an additional, avoidable social relationship and not doing so, they more often veer towards not doing so; hence why so few wanted to involve a third party by making any transfer at all in the Dictator

Game. If this view is roughly right, then it is a great lesson in the value of multiple methods. If we had just had the Dictator Game, or only the observational data, then we would have come to very different and much less nuanced generalizations about prosociality in the two neighbourhoods.

There were still other measures of prosociality that we gathered, in the form of small, naturalistic field assays: dropping lost letters, asking people for directions, asking people for change, and dropping objects like pens and keys in the street. I like these simple measures because they are more naturalistic than the economic games, and closer to the flow of behaviour on the streets than the surveys are. The results (presented in detail in Nettle et al., 2011) were quite illuminating in view of the foregoing discussion. For the lost letters, there was a huge neighbourhood difference: they pretty much all came home from neighbourhood A, with very few from Neighbourhood B. On the other hand, in the cases of asking directions, making change, or dropping an object, there were no discernible neighbourhood differences, despite considerable care taken to perform the assay in a standardized way. There could be banal explanations for this pattern, such as the fact that lost letters may disappear amongst the litter that is a depressing feature of the streets of B. Equally, though, they could relate to the patterns we have already discussed. With the lost letter, passers-by have to decide whether to become momentarily involved in the affairs of some person unknown, by picking up their letter and posting it. What if it turns out to contain something illegal, controversial, or nefarious? You are now implicated because you handled it. If you feel that others around you are close to the edge, and might therefore be sending all kinds of strange letters, it might be better to walk on by without anyone noticing. By contrast, in asking directions and making change, you can't walk on by: you have already been accosted, and thus you have no real choice but to follow the social interaction to some kind of ending. And once you are part of the social interaction, you might as well be helpful, because whatever state your interlocutor is in, they are going to prefer helpfulness. This interpretation does not, admittedly, explain the lack of neighbourhood difference for the dropped object, which would appear to be more like the lost letter in that the participant can plausibly walk on by without initiating any social interaction. But it does suggest why the lost letter patterns with the Dictator Game, whilst asking for directions and making change do not.

4. Crime and punishment

Broken glass, everywhere.
People pissing on the stairs; you know they just don't care.

Introduction

Where the previous chapter was about helping one another, this chapter is about the harms we can do. That is, we are concerned in this chapter with neighbourhood patterns of antisocial acts, acts that are to the detriment of another person or group. Prosocial and antisocial behaviour are logically distinct but nonetheless connected. It is not logically necessary that when people are less inclined to help each other, they will be more inclined to do each other harm, but in practice this often seems to be true. We have two sets of reasons for expecting there to be a greater prevalence of antisocial behaviour in Neighbourhood B than A.

First, there is the edge principle discussed in the previous chapter. I claimed that people in Neighbourhood B tend on average, as a consequence of deprivation, to be closer to the existential edge than those in A, and hence to be more likely to be pushed to the edge itself. When you are on the edge, risky options for solving your immediate problem start to look attractive, because their payoff is often immediate, and their best possible payoff is often enormously advantageous to the actor (though since they are risky, their best possible payoff is not their most likely payoff). The kinds of risky options that might present themselves to people in difficulty in a modern city include lying, robbery, stealing from individuals, or coercing others to change their behaviour. These are all antisocial acts. Indeed, to act

  http://dx.doi.org/10.11647/OBP.0084.04

antisocially can be considered as putting a higher valuation on the short-term maximal payoff of the act than on the possible negative consequences, some of which might be subtle (loss of reputation or friendship, for example), and many of which are deferred in time.

The second reason for expecting greater antisocial behaviour in B is empirical. Previous research has established very clearly that neighbourhoods where social capital is low are also those where crime tends to be high, and crime is the archetypal antisocial behaviour (Sampson et al., 1997). Crucially, social capital in these studies is measured in much the way we measured it in Social Survey 1, via self-report surveys. Given the neighbourhood difference in self-reported social capital reviewed in chapter 3, the clear prediction should be that antisocial behaviour in all its forms will be more prevalent in B than A. This is also what the Mountain People narrative leads us to expect.

The spreading of disorder and the maintenance of antisocial behaviour

This chapter is about more than just whether there is neighbourhood difference in antisocial behaviour; that would be relatively quick to demonstrate. It is about using our neighbourhood study to try to understand the forces though which patterns of antisocial behaviour are maintained and transmitted. For what is absolutely clear is that antisocial behaviour is a transmissible condition. I mentioned Keizer, Lindenberg and Steg's experiments in chapter 1. Those experiments showed that antisocial rule-breaking behaviours can be increased in a field setting by sowing the environment with small cues that other people are already being antisocial, such as graffiti or litter (Keizer et al., 2008). This 'spreading of disorder' principle is a powerful one. It lies behind the 'broken windows' theory of crime, which asserts that allowing relatively small antisocial acts to remain visible in the environment leads to increases in much more serious crime. The outputs of the small antisocial acts—the broken windows and graffitied walls—come to serve as informational inputs to other potential perpetrators, whose behaviour in turn serves as the input to others, and so on in an escalating cycle.

What interests me most about the spreading of disorder principle is its potential to make antisocial behaviour inflationary and self-perpetuating. Let us say that there is a small initial difference between two neighbourhoods;

maybe there is one desperate person who goes around despoiling the public street in one of them but not the other. His acts serve as inputs to other decision-makers, who then are more prepared to commit small antisocial acts of their own; those in turn infect people contemplating more serious destruction, and before we know it one neighbourhood is obviously disordered—and has a high crime rate—and the other not. Even if we now remove the person who was the initial source of the disorder, the difference may persist. The experiences of the people in the two neighbourhoods have become different enough to lead them to choose different behaviours, and those different behaviours in turn feed into the experiences of their peers. Thus, the result could be a kind of pluralistic ignorance, where even if *everyone* in the neighbourhood has a preference not to behave antisocially, they all make the inductive bet—because of the overwhelming evidence around them—that *other* inhabitants are antisocial, and so they may as well follow suit. Thus, a small initial difference in neighbourhood conditions could lead to a rather large difference in outcomes, one with the potential to perpetuate itself indefinitely without counteracting forces.

There may be counteracting forces, of course. They can come from prosocial behaviour, explaining the intimate link between absence of prosociality and presence of antisociality. Where people are prosocially inclined, they will be willing to invest in small acts of order restoration, like clearing up litter even if they did not cause it, or repairing a window that they did not break, and they will be seen doing so. Thus, visible prosocial acts can neutralize or reverse the self-reinforcing cycle (Keizer, Lindenberg, & Steg, 2013). Another way that prosocial behaviour can be a brake on the spreading of disorder is through third-party sanctioning. Third parties will often intervene, at cost to themselves, where they see antisocial acts occur. This can take various forms, the simplest of which is the social embarrassment of the perpetrator, but it provides some kind of deterrent. Third-party sanctioning can be thought of as a kind of prosociality, since it provides a specific benefit to the victim of the act and, through deterrence, a more diffuse benefit to the community. Where social capital is higher, people are more willing to sanction, and this is an important brake on the spreading of disorder.

In light of the foregoing discussion, we can therefore make several predictions concerning antisocial behaviour in Neighbourhoods A and B. First, there will be more of it in B, and it will span both minor acts such as littering and more serious criminal acts; according to the 'broken windows' theory of crime, minor and more serious types of antisocial behaviour should go together. Second, the spreading of disorder principle says that increased antisocial behaviour in B should be substantially mediated by a perception that *other* people in the neighbourhood are being antisocial; take this perception away, and the neighbourhood difference should be much smaller. Finally, given the lower social capital, we should expect less willingness to prosocially sanction wrongdoers in B. This should heighten the difference in antisocial behaviour. We will now scrutinize the data from the Tyneside Neighbourhoods Project to examine whether these predictions are supported.

Littering and crime reports

The simplest place to start is littering in Observational Dataset 1. I coded a number of things that could be considered markers of antisocial behaviour. There was *littering* (dropping refuse to the ground) and its mirror image, *bin* (disposing of refuse in a designated on-street refuse container). A category of *damaging* recorded anyone apparently trying to break with hands or stones, or set fire to, the street furniture, a vehicle, or a building. Finally, *spitting* could perhaps be considered a kind of antisocial behaviour, since it is presumably convenient to the spitter but would be considered by many to negatively affect the hygiene of the environment.

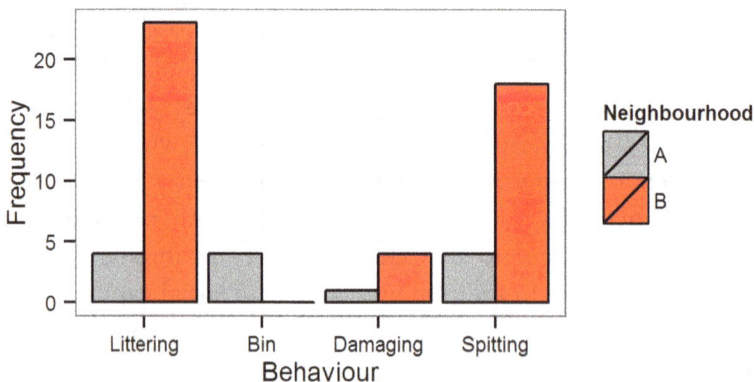

Figure 4.1 Frequency of markers of antisocial behaviour by neighbourhood, from Observational Dataset 1. Bin is strictly speaking a marker of prosocial rather than antisocial behaviour, and it is the only marker to pattern in the opposite direction. Image © Daniel Nettle, CC BY.

As Figure 4.1 shows, there were large neighbourhood differences in all of the markers of antisocial behaviour, though the absolute numbers of acts observed were small in some cases. I saw littering six times as often in B than A; about every 31 minutes of observation, as opposed to every 3 hours. Relatedly, I never saw anyone put anything into a bin in B, though I saw it 4 times in A, and street bins are widely available in both neighbourhoods. These figures refer to acts of dropping litter. I am sure that a survey of litter already on the ground would reveal a huge neighbourhood difference too. Acts of damaging were fortunately rare, but stacked up 4-1 for Neighbourhood B. Finally, spitting was over four times as frequent in B as A. Note that the total number of people observed was reasonably similar in the two neighbourhoods, so these differences are not just a product of different opportunities for observation.

That tells us a lot about minor antisocial acts; is there a neighbourhood difference in crime too? Agathe's police dataset recorded all incidents notified to the police over the period December 2010 to March 2011, 585 incidents in all. There were 385 in B to 200 in A, a ratio of 1.93. Figure 4.2 categorizes these by type of incident, showing also the ratio of the number of incidents in B to the number in A.

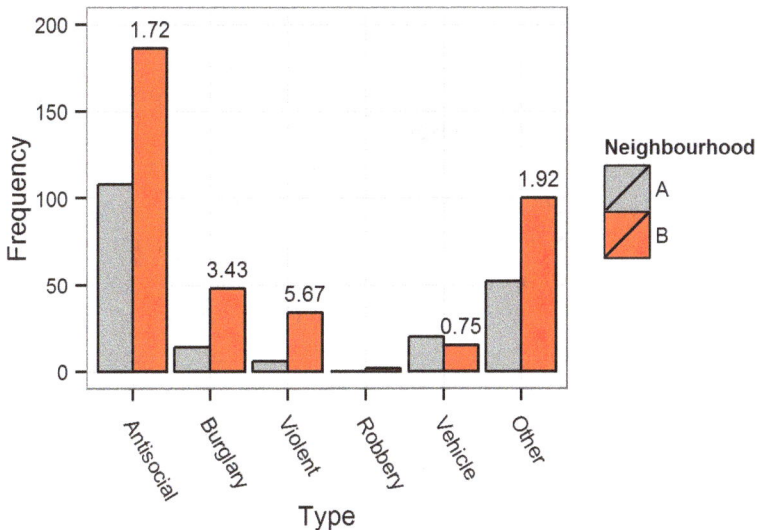

Figure 4.2 Crime rates by type and neighbourhood from the Police Crime Dataset. The figures on the Neighbourhood B bars give the ratio of the number of incidents of the type in B to the number in A. Antisocial denotes minor incidents of public nuisance. Image © Daniel Nettle, CC BY.

The only category of crime for which Neighbourhood B does not show an elevated rate is vehicle crime. This is unsurprising since there are fewer and less valuable vehicles in B. Other categories show at least 70% more incidents in B than A. This includes a greater incidence of what the police describe as antisocial behaviour, a category that refers to disputes, littering, and graffiti, among others. This is consistent with the evidence from Observational Dataset 1. Of particular note in Figure 4.2 are two things: burglaries are much more common in B than A, even though the monetary value of the households is surely much lower. Naively, you might predict that A would be the more attractive place for burglars to ply their trade. Secondly, the biggest neighbourhood difference of all is in violence. Crime overall is slightly less than twice as common in B than A; violence is nearly six times as common. The pattern we observed in Neighbourhood B is apparently typical of extremely deprived neighbourhoods: an excess of crime overall, and a particularly large excess of violent crime (Krivo & Peterson, 1996).

These findings relate to several claims I have already made. I claimed that people in Neighbourhood B are more likely to be close to the edge than those in A. The fact that there are many more burglaries and robberies in B than A reinforces this point. Most burglaries are performed close to the perpetrator's home (Bernasco & Nieuwbeerta, 2005). Thus, most of these crimes are probably committed by people from in and around the neighbourhood. As well as being very risky, they are probably not very lucrative. These are acts of people who are close to the edge. We have already seen the example of the men who robbed their own bookmaker in chapter 3. To take another example, an off-licence close to Neighbourhood B was robbed on May 8th, 2011 by a man with a large knife. He made off with two packets of cigarettes and a bar of chocolate, a total value of less than £20. He was arrested outside the shop. Only to a person at or over the edge could the possibility of £20 worth of chocolate and cigarettes outweigh the reasonably large chance of a prison term.

The finding that violence is so much more common in B relates to the claim I made in chapter 3 about social relationships in B being more volatile over time than those in A. We don't have much detail about these violent incidents or why they happened. However, we know that most violence happens between people who know each other, and so at the very least we can say that its greater prevalence indicates that social relationships in B more often take the most extreme swing possible to the negative. Even if this is rare in absolute terms, it is much more likely to happen in Neighbourhood B than A.

The Theft Game

The observational and police datasets are useful for telling us what people do, but they give us no real window onto why they do them. That is, they provide no way of investigating the cognitive processes underlying the decision to behave antisocially, since they do not furnish the opportunity to asking the litterers or criminals anything. Thus, a different method was required. We needed to recruit participants from Neighbourhoods A and B, offer them the opportunity to behave antisocially, and explore the cognitive and situational determinants of their decisions. Economic games were going to be the way to do this.

This part of the project was Kari Britt Schroeder's work. I described in chapter 1 the economic game she designed that was attached to Social Survey 2. Briefly, players were formed into mutually anonymous triads. There was an initial allocation of £10 to each player. Player 1 could decide to 'steal' up to £10 from player 2, thus increasing his earnings to a maximum of £20. The unfortunate player 2 could not do anything about this. Player 3, however, could decide to sanction player 1 for his behaviour, by paying £2 to reduce player 1's take-home amount by £6. At the time player 3 was filling in her survey, she did not yet know what player 1 had decided to do, so what we obtained from player 3 was a series of choices: if player 1 takes £0, would you fine him? If player 1 takes £1, would you fine him? etc. Thus, we ended up, for each triad, with a look-up table of what to do in terms of final payouts for every possible player 1 decision about how much to steal.

The player 1 decisions are an assay of willingness to commit antisocial behaviour. From the rest of Social Survey 2, we had data from those same player 1s about their perceptions of norms concerning social cheating. The questions Kari asked to probe perceived norms were about three domains of real-world antisocial behaviour: cheating on benefits, cheating on taxes, and cheating on public transport fares. We asked both about injunctive norms or acceptability (to what extent is it acceptable to cheat in this way?) and descriptive norms or prevalence (how much do people in this neighbourhood actually cheat in this way?). These norms ratings were on an effectively arbitrary continuous scale. The spreading of disorder principle predicts that the greater player 1's perception of the prevalence of cheating in the neighbourhood, the more she will steal from player 2. It does not predict any association between the amount player 1 steals and her rating of the acceptability of social cheating, though common sense would make this prediction. So many findings in the social sciences are intuitively obvious: it is nice in this case to have a theoretical prediction that does not completely coincide with intuition. Unreflective intuition would say that people who think social cheating is less acceptable will steal less, whereas the spreading of disorder principle suggests that people who think others around them are cheating less will steal less. These are not mutually exclusive of course, but it was interesting to investigate which one panned out.

Let us look at the results for the player 1s (Figure 4.3; I have plotted these in a different way from Kari's more sophisticated analysis in Schroeder, Pepper, and Nettle [2014]). First, player 1s behaved differently in the two neighbourhoods. The top left panel of Figure 4.3 is what is called a violin plot. It shows how the data (the amounts stolen) are distributed across their possible range of £0 to £10. Where the violin is wide, there are many observations, and where it is narrow, there are few. As you can see, in Neighbourhood A the violin is wide at £0. This means that most people stole £0; this is reinforced by the fact that the median amount stolen (black dot) is £0. There is a very thin neck in the middle of the range, meaning very few people stole an amount like £5, and a little bulge at the top, representing a small number of people who stole everything. The violin for Neighbourhood B is quite different. The bulge at zero is not so pronounced; there were many fewer people who stole nothing. There are more marked bulges in the middle and at the top, meaning that many more people stole half or everything. This is reinforced by the fact that the median theft for Neighbourhood B was £5. In other words, the middle person of the people we sampled in A took nothing from player 2; the middle person of the people we sampled in B took half of what there was to take. The neighbourhood difference was robust to controlling for the subjective value of a few pounds, as well as obvious covariates such as age and sex.

The upper right panel of Figure 4.3 shows how rated acceptability and prevalence of social cheating compare across the neighbourhoods. There is no real neighbourhood difference in the ratings of acceptability. Respondents from both places thought that social cheating was pretty unacceptable. There was, however, a huge difference in the perceived prevalence: respondents from B thought that social cheating was much more common in their neighbourhood. This matters, because of what the lower two panels of Figure 4.3 show. There was no relationship between how much player 1s took in the game and how acceptable they regarded social cheating as being (lower left panel). This is very striking and, as mentioned above, unintuitive: people who a few minutes later went on to take all £10 rated social cheating as just as unacceptable as people who went on to take nothing. By contrast, there was a relationship between perceived prevalence of social cheating and amount taken: the more common you regard social cheating as being in your neighbourhood, the more you take from poor old player 2. The neighbourhood difference in the perceived prevalence of social cheating, it turns out, largely explains the neighbourhood difference in how much of the £10 player 1 took.

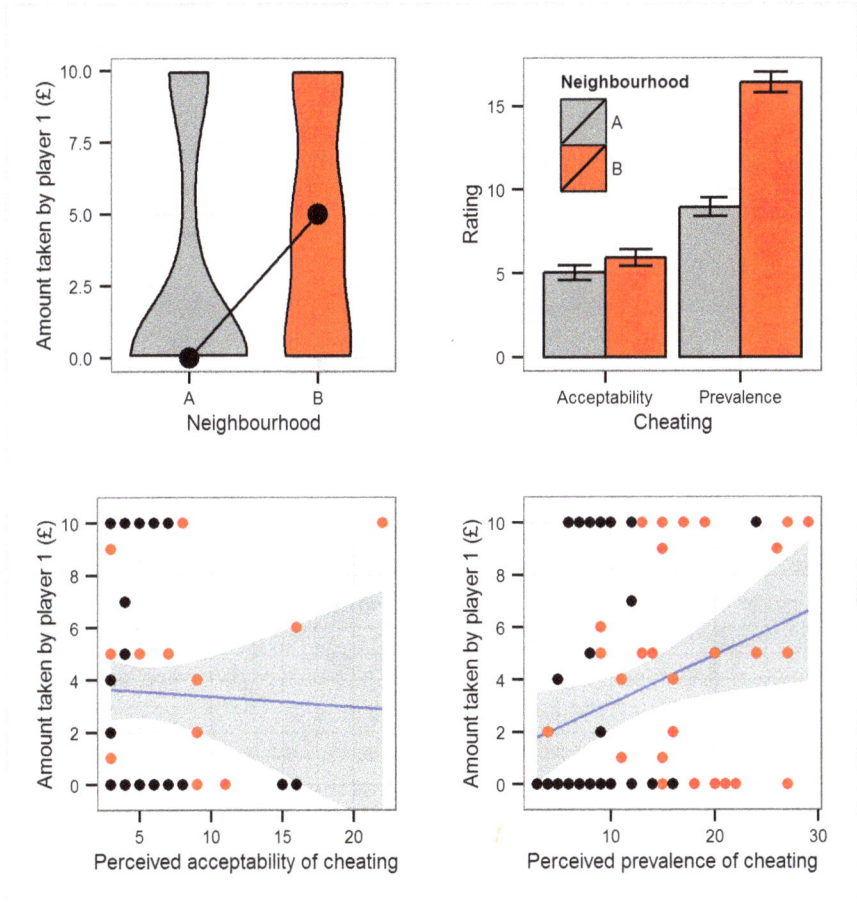

Figure 4.3 Upper left: Violin plot of amount taken by player 1s in the Theft Game by neighbourhood. The black points are the medians. The curved shape represents the distribution of the data symmetrically on an arbitrary horizontal scale; where the shape is wide, there are many observations, whilst where it is narrow there are few. Upper right: Mean ratings of acceptability of social cheating, and prevalence of social cheating, by neighbourhood. Error bars represent one standard error. Bottom left: Scatterplot of the relationship between acceptability of social cheating and amount taken in the game. Bottom right: Scatterplot of the relationship between perceived prevalence of social cheating in the neighbourhood and amount taken in the game. Image © Daniel Nettle, CC BY.

These results resonate with our expectations. For one thing, they support the general claim, backed up by much empirical research, that normative influence is very important (Cialdini, Reno, & Kallgren, 1990). Under a range of circumstances, people are prone to doing as much or as little as they perceive others in the surrounding population to be doing. Normative influences are often much stronger than people realize; respondents protest that such influences are unimportant and that they base their decisions on more elaborate and independent criteria, such as values or extensive reasoning. The behavioural evidence tends to suggest otherwise (Nolan, Schultz, Cialdini, Goldstein, & Griskevicius, 2008). The results also confirm the more specific prediction of the spreading of disorder principle: the more the participants felt they saw evidence of cheating going on around them, the more they stole. This is really just the importance of normative influence applied to antisocial behaviour in particular.

We now turn to player 3. What is she doing in all this? Recall that we predicted people in Neighbourhood A might be more willing than those in B to sanction antisocial behaviours, even when they were not the injured party. This did indeed turn out to be the case (Figure 4.4). The figure shows the proportion of player 3s from each neighbourhood saying that they would impose the fine, for each of the possible amounts that player 1 might steal from player 2. In both neighbourhoods, there was a sense of graduated sanction. That is, most people would let pass a small theft of a pound or two, but as the theft became bigger, more and more of them said that they would intercede. The proportion opting to sanction never approached 1 in either neighbourhood; there were plenty of people who were simply not going to get involved. However, the proportion not willing to get involved was much higher in Neighbourhood B than A, and as a consequence, the probability of getting fined increased less as the amount player 1 stole got larger. In Neighbourhood B, even a player 1 who stole the whole £10 was more likely to get away with it than not.

What explains the greater willingness to sanction in Neighbourhood A than B? People in Neighbourhood A reported greater trust and did not rate so highly the value of the £2 the fine cost them. Both trust and the subjective value of £2 were important in predicting people's willingness to sanction (specifically, willingness to sanction was greater where the subjective value of £2 was low, and amongst those for whom the subjective value of £2 was low, willingness to sanction increased with trust of the neighbours).

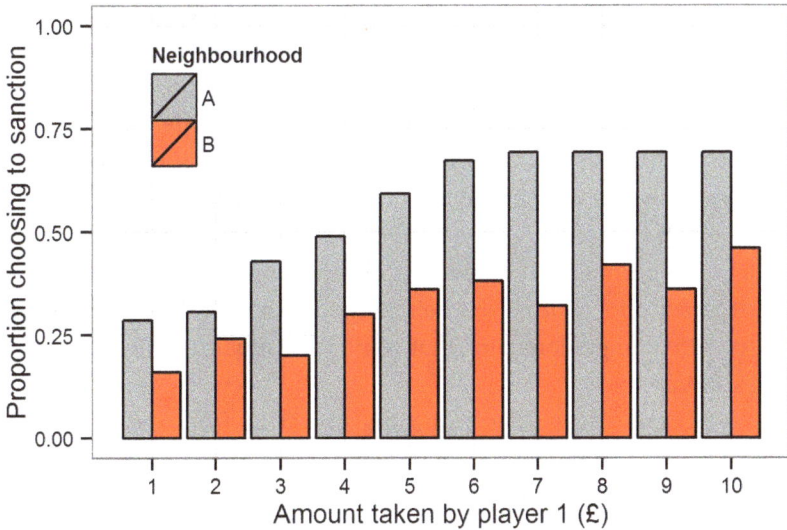

Figure 4.4 The proportion of player 3 respondents in each neighbourhood opting to sanction each possible amount stolen by player 1. Image © Daniel Nettle, CC BY.

The combination of variation in the subjective value of £2 and variation in trust was sufficient to explain the neighbourhood variation in sanctioning behaviour. These results suggest that people will intercede on behalf of third parties when it is not too costly for them to do so, and when they trust that they are part of a viable prosocial network. Interceding is after all a kind of prosociality, and so, like other kinds of prosociality, we are more willing to embark on it when we have confidence in the social entity within which it will occur.

An experiment with information

The data from Kari's study that I have presented so far shows a clear association between willingness to behave antisocially and the perception that others behave antisocially (that is, the perceived descriptive norm). However, the claim we wanted to make was stronger than just an association: we wanted to argue that perceived descriptive norms play a *causal* role in maintaining greater antisocial behaviour in Neighbourhood

B than A. Demonstrating causality is a challenge. Surveys are informative, but the general consensus is that only experiments (randomised control trials, if you prefer) can really tell you anything very firm about cause and effect. An experiment in this context would mean a study where participants were randomly assigned to experience different descriptive norms about cheating in their neighbourhoods. If the association is causal, their antisocial behaviour should then vary according to the norm they were assigned to. Of course, it is rather difficult without vast resources to think of a way of experimentally assigning different participants to experience different descriptive norms in their neighbourhoods. Nonetheless, Kari came up with an ingenious plan that went at least part of the way towards a true experiment.

The experiment was done using the player 2s from the Theft Game described in the preceding section. Recall that the unfortunate player 2 had no active decision to make in the game; he or she was the potential victim of player 1's theft. However, we did ask player 2s whether or not they expected player 3 to come to their aid and punish player 1 in the event that player 1 stole £5 from them. Expecting player 3 to come to your aid is not the same thing as stealing, of course, but it is related to it. Presumably if people in a neighbourhood began to expect more sanctioning by third parties, their willingness to commit antisocial behaviour would be reduced. Thus, we in effect used the player 2 expectations about sanctioning as a marker for the perceived extent to which antisocial behaviour could be got away with.

Now, how could we experimentally manipulate people's experience of descriptive norms in the neighbourhood? Other studies have done this by, for example, deliberately littering in some areas or on some days (Cialdini et al., 1990). However, this was difficult to do for a study on a whole-neighbourhood scale taking place over several months. Instead what we did is a really rather subtle manipulation of the social information available to the participants. We acquire our beliefs about descriptive norms at least partly through social communication; we are influenced by what others say the norms are. So we decided to present some player 2s in B with information that implied other residents thought the neighbourhood descriptive norms were not as bad as they really were; we also presented some participants in A with information implying that other residents thought the neighbourhood descriptive norms were worse than they actually were. We called this the norms treatment: in the norms treatment groups, you got information implying that your neighbours thought *your* neighbourhood was more like the *other* neighbourhood was in reality. These participants were to be compared to two control groups who received no information at all about what other residents thought about the local descriptive norms. The clear prediction was that perceptions of the probability of player 3 sanctioning would be shifted: in A, the norms treatment should reduce the perceived probability of sanctioning, whilst in B, the norms treatment should increase it.

The details of how to implement the norms treatment were quite involved. As mentioned in chapter 2, for ethical reasons, Kari did not want to give people false information, but she did have to manipulate their informational state. She thus decided on the following solution: in the norms treatment, instead of the questions asking for ratings of the prevalence of cheating on taxes, benefits, and public transport fares in the neighbourhood, player 2s would see a statement informing them that we had asked ten of their neighbours what *they* thought about these issues, and showing the average results. We really had asked ten people in each neighbourhood, of course, so what the participants saw were real data. In fact, we had asked many more than ten. The experimental manipulation consisted in the fact that the ten we chose to present were unrepresentative: ten of the *most* favourable for Neighbourhood B, and ten of the *least* favourable for Neighbourhood A. We hoped that receiving this biased social information would cause people to shift their own representations of what the descriptive norms concerning cheating were in the neighbourhood.

The results from the norms manipulation are shown in Figure 4.5. In the control conditions, respondents from B were slightly less likely than those from A to expect player 3 to intercede on their behalf. This difference does have a basis in reality, since player 3s from B really were less likely to intercede. However, in the norms condition for Neighbourhood B, the expectation of player 3 sanctioning was strikingly higher—around 60% as opposed to around 30% for the controls. One of our predictions was thus fulfilled. The other prediction was that the proportion expecting sanctioning should be reduced by the norms treatment in Neighbourhood A. There was no evidence for this. In fact, the proportion of respondents expecting sanctioning was slightly higher in the norms condition than the control for Neighbourhood A.

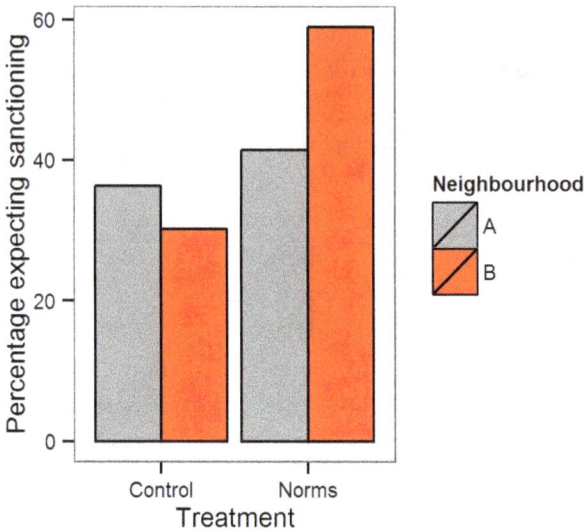

Figure 4.5 The percentage of player 2 participants expecting that player 3 would sanction player 1 if player 1 stole £5, by neighbourhood and experimental treatment. The norms treatment is described in the text. Image © Daniel Nettle, CC BY.

These results are really very striking. For Neighbourhood B at any rate, they confirm the causal importance of perceived norms in cognition concerning prosocial and antisocial behaviour. They also show how strong the social transmission of these perceived norms is. Just by telling people that their neighbours thought that the neighbourhood was a slightly less antisocial place than the behavioural evidence suggests it is, you could effectively and instantly double people's expectations that a stranger would intercede to sanction antisocial behaviour. And if residents' expectations that antisocial behaviour would get sanctioned could be doubled, you would instantly provide a massive deterrent effect against antisocial behaviour itself. Thus, our experiment suggested that the apparently entrenched antisocial culture of Neighbourhood B might actually be quite labile: you just needed to persuade everyone in B that everyone *else* in B was motivated to be prosocial and not antisocial. It would become a self-fulfilling prophecy.

This finding relates to the issue discussed at the outset of the chapter about how the spreading of disorder principle means that antisocial cultures can be self-sustaining. Once people start to believe that others in the surrounding community are on the lookout for themselves and not doing their bit for the common good, they will behave accordingly. Their behavioural output becomes perceptual input to their fellow community members, and so the loop is hermetically closed. The cultural tradition can persist even if whatever perturbation initially gave rise to it has been removed. Our Neighbourhood B results suggest that perhaps quite small and simple things might break the loop quite quickly: getting neighbours to talk to each other positively about the places where they live; volunteer days where people could see each other doing prosocial acts; deep community clean-up to remove the visible cues of disorder. Other experimental work with manipulations of perceived norms suggests that the effects of such interventions could be quite powerful (Cialdini et al., 1990; Keizer et al., 2008, 2013).

Before we conclude that our results show that community regeneration is going to be straightforward and require only superficial nudges, some caveats are in order. First, the shift in expectations of sanctioning that we achieved in Neighbourhood B in this experiment may well have been quite fleeting. We have no idea if there would still be an effect if we had asked respondents a week or even a day later. I suspect not; the thing about real-world experience is that it is happening all the time. One particular set of cues might be influential in the short term, but it will soon be overwritten by others. The second is a more general point. The chances are that what maintains the relatively antisocial culture of B is not *just* the social transmission effect whereby everyone does what they think everyone else is doing. There are also more people who are materially desperate, as I made clear in the discussion of the edge principle in chapter 3. People at or over an edge will sometimes do antisocial things regardless of what they perceive the local descriptive norm to be. Thus, breaking the cycle of social transmission might well ameliorate the neighbourhood difference in the short term, but it is always going to be in danger of breaking out again if the underlying socioeconomic issues are not addressed. I return to this issue in chapter 7.

The strange case of the norms effect that didn't happen

There is an aspect of the results of Kari's norms experiment that I have glossed over thus far: the complete failure of the norms treatment to produce the predicted result in Neighbourhood A. Being given information suggesting that the neighbours thought A was less prosocial than it actually is did *not* reduce the expectation of sanctioning. That expectation was if anything slightly higher in the norms treatment than in the control. In addition, a curious and unpredicted thing happened. Participants from A who received the norms treatment did not seem to want our money. Six of them spontaneously opted out of receiving the payment from the game: three suggested we donate it to charity, two told us to keep it for university funds, and one just said he did not want to receive it. Only one person in the Neighbourhood A control condition deflected payment in this way, so it seems like something may be going on.

One interpretation of these findings is as follows. People in Neighbourhood A *know* that it is a nice and prosocial place. They are not under any uncertainty about that, and so their beliefs are relatively immune from moment-to-moment influence. Strictly speaking, in information theory, the amount of information carried by a signal depends on the extent of the uncertainty in the receiver (Shannon, 1948). Our Neighbourhood A respondents were not uncertain, and so the cues we provided were not informative and did not lead to them updating their expectations. All the Neighbourhood A respondents did was to signal to us that *we* were wrong, demonstrating what a prosocial bunch the residents of A are by spontaneously transforming our economic game into an opportunity for charitable giving. Not only did they not heed the social information we provided in the norms treatment; six of them sought to actively *counter* it by a well-chosen prosocial gesture.

The corollary interpretation for Neighbourhood B is that people there are in considerable uncertainty about the state of the social world. Thus, even the rather subtle cue that we fed them carried considerable information, and their running representations shifted markedly. This relates to the finding reported in chapter 3 that residents of B feel they know their neighbours less well, even though they demonstrably interact with them more frequently, than residents of A do. That finding showed that residents of B feel that they need more information about their social world; the current one suggests that they are responsive to it when it comes. I suggested in chapter 3 that the difference in information-hunger is to do with people's behaviour being more variable over time in B than A, and the same claim works for the information-reactivity we see here. When behaviour is variable, more data are more useful. Moreover, you need to give a strong weight to the most *recent* data, since that is what is most diagnostic about the current state of affairs. In an unchanging environment, you can give a lot of weight to your historical experience, but in a volatile environment, historical experience means little; it is the most recent data that are going to be of some help. Thus, residents of B may be the most tuned for any news or evidence going around of how social behaviour in the neighbourhoods is shifting. Interestingly, this suggests that it may be in disordered or deprived neighbourhoods where you could have the most dramatic short-term effects from interventions like clearing up litter or mending broken windows.

5. From cradle to grave

A child is born with no state of mind,
Blind to the ways of mankind.

Introduction

Chapters 3 and 4 showed that adults' social lives are very obviously different in Neighbourhood B than in Neighbourhood A. Residents of Neighbourhood B interact more with their neighbours, but trust them less. A question we can ask is how these neighbourhood differences are patterned across the life course. For example, is the social behaviour of children initially the same across neighbourhoods, with differences only becoming apparent once people have grown up? Or is the social world of young children different in different neighbourhoods from the earliest age at which we can measure it? How different are children's experiences in the different neighbourhoods, and how does this relate to adults' lives? These questions are the subject of this chapter. First, we will go back to the Observational Datasets and look specifically at the behaviour of the children on the streets, trying to understand how that differs by neighbourhood, and how the differences in child social behaviour relate to the corresponding differences in the adults. The next part of the chapter will be devoted to understanding how trust—which as we have already seen is a key indicator of social capital and prosocial motivation—varies with age. Finally, we will look at the behaviour of older people through the Street Ages Dataset.

 http://dx.doi.org/10.11647/OBP.0084.05

Children's use of the streets

Using Observational Dataset 1, we can ask for children the same question that we asked in chapter 3 for adults: how do they use the streets across the day? Figure 5.1 shows the numbers of children (i.e. people judged to be of compulsory school age—16 or younger) observed in main and residential streets by time of day. Children are generally more in evidence in Neighbourhood B than A. This is particularly true in the residential streets in the evening. You can see the clear spike in numbers of children as the school days end around 15:00. In Neighbourhood A, they continue to be around in some numbers until 18:00, whereupon they presumably go in for their dinners. Thereafter very few are seen. In Neighbourhood B by contrast, children come to play out in the evening and in large numbers. Of course, they could be playing outside in Neighbourhood A too, just within the confines of their larger gardens, but it is not my impression that this is the case. Playing out on the streets is certainly a rarity in Neighbourhood A relative to B. An important point here is that playing out is playing social: of the 290 groups containing a child observed on the streets after 18:00 in B, 59% contained more than one child, and 33% contained more than two.

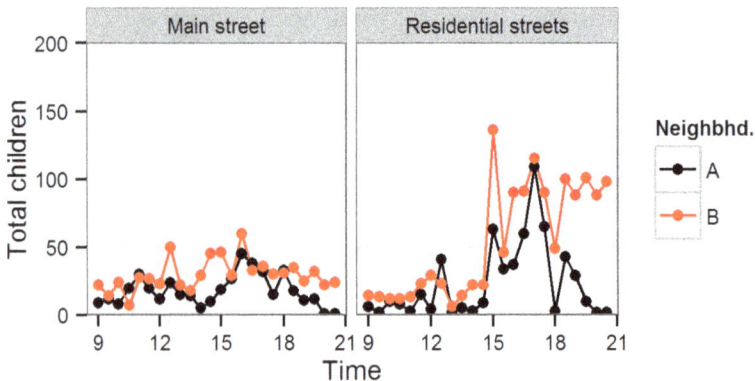

Figure 5.1   Total numbers of children on the streets by time of day in Observational Dataset 1. Image © Daniel Nettle, CC BY.

The pattern for the adults was that individuals in Neighbourhood B were less likely to be on their own than individuals in Neighbourhood A. Does this also hold for the children? Figure 5.2 shows the proportion of groups containing children in which there is just one child, two children, or more than two children. One-child groups are indeed relatively less common in B than A, two-child groups are also fractionally less common, and the more-than-two category is overrepresented. The groups in this category were sometimes large, containing up to 12 or 15 children. They use the streets to play traditional children's games, or cards, or football, or they stand around and talk. Given UK patterns of family size, few of these large groups can consist only of siblings. Instead, the data suggest that children in B use the public space for greater social interaction with other children from other households.

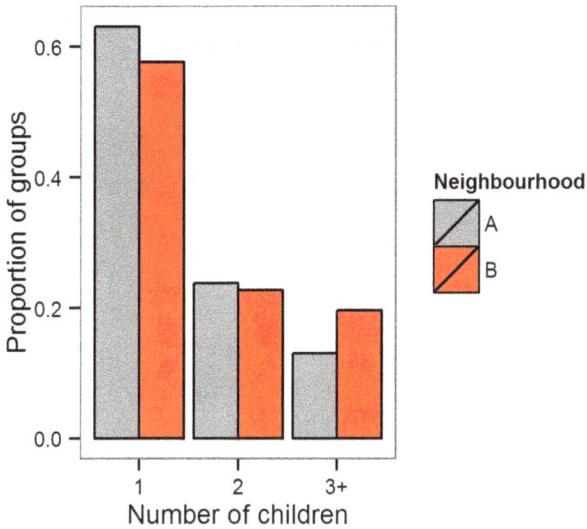

Figure 5.2 The proportion of groups containing children with different numbers of children, by neighbourhood, from Observational Dataset 1. Image © Daniel Nettle, CC BY.

What adults are accompanying these groups? The left panel of Figure 5.3 shows the number of adults found in the social groups containing children, by neighbourhood. Two things are striking about this graph. First, children are much more likely to be unaccompanied by any adult in Neighbourhood B. This relates to the greater frequency of playing out in B, since playing out is something usually done by children on their own; of the 290 evening residential-street children's groups in Neighbourhood B, 175 were adult-free. The second striking feature is that mixed adult/ children groups in Neighbourhood B are more likely to have multiple adults in them than equivalent groups in A. Children going about Neighbourhood A are most likely to be with exactly one adult; children going about Neighbourhood B are about equally likely to be with no adult, one adult, or more than one adult.

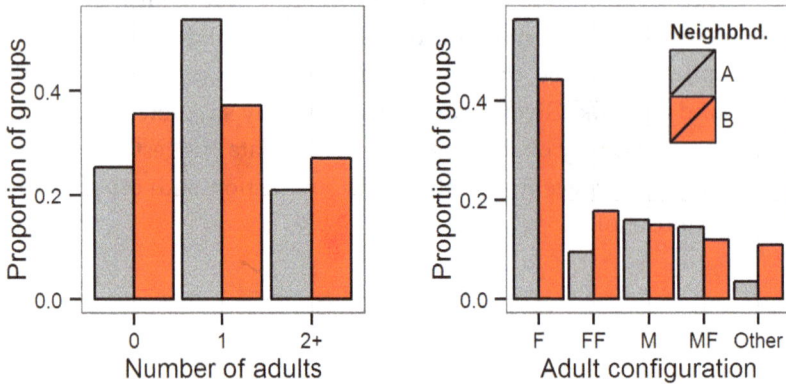

Figure 5.3 For each neighbourhood in Observational Dataset 1: (left) the distribution of the number of adults found in social groups containing children; (right) the proportion of mixed adult/children groups constituted by different configurations of adults. Image © Daniel Nettle, CC BY.

We can drill down further into the configurations of adults accompanying children. The right panel of Figure 5.3 only examines groups which contain at least one adult and at least one child, and divides them up according to the configuration of adults present. As you can see, a large proportion of all adult/children groups in both neighbourhoods have one female as the sole adult. However, the predominance of this group type is substantially lessened in Neighbourhood B compared to A. The difference is not made up by an increase in lone male-headed groups, or 'mum and dad' groups. Instead, in B, there are proportionally more groups with two adult women, and more groups belonging to the 'other' category. This category represents all kinds of constellations of multiple men and women; there were 47 groups with 3 adults in Neighbourhood B (as against 9 in A), and 29 groups with 4 or more (as against 7 in A).

How do we interpret these patterns? First, children are more socially autonomous in Neighbourhood B than A, as their greater propensity to be without adults and to be playing out demonstrates. Depending on your views you could see this as a danger: lack of parental supervision is the pathway to delinquency. On the other hand, you could see it is a positive: young people in Neighbourhood B have earlier opportunities to become independent social actors in the neighbourhood and create their own social networks. And they do. Children in B are less likely to be the lone child in a group and—we can reasonably infer—more likely to be on the streets with children from other households. Second, whereas children's social behaviour in A is largely organized through the nuclear grouping of one woman and her one or two children, the groupings are more varied and larger in B. They will more often contain a pair of women and their multiple children, or some more complex set of adults and children. In short, the data suggest that children in B, as well as having more interaction with other children across household boundaries, are also having more interaction with the adults from other households too, via multi-family social aggregations. The adult Neighbourhood B pattern of greater social interaction on the streets therefore shapes, and is reproduced in, the social experience of children.

Social trust through childhood

In the adult data, there is a paradox: the greater social interaction across household boundaries in the deprived Neighbourhood B does not lead to higher social trust, as common sense would predict it should, but actually goes hand in hand with lower social trust. We have seen that children are involved in greater social interaction in Neighbourhood B; do they also trust less?

We can't exactly answer this question, since we don't have data on children's trust from Neighbourhoods A and B. However, we do have data on social trust from the School Survey. To recall, this survey was from around 1000 school students from 8 Tyneside neighbourhoods other than A and B. On the deprivation continuum, the most deprived was not quite as deprived as B, the least deprived about the same as A, and there were a few in between. Thus, having social trust data from these neighbourhoods is an interesting potential corroboration of the association between deprivation and low trust, and may also tell us something about trust patterns in childhood.

Social trust was measured in the School Survey with a standard question and a response on a 1 (not at all) to 100 (completely) scale. To display the data, I have split the responses by age group, and also by the Index of Multiple Deprivation of the neighbourhood (Figure 5.4). Note that a higher Index of Multiple Deprivation represents greater deprivation. As you can see, in all three age groups there is a social gradient in trust, with average trust lower as the neighbourhoods become more deprived. It is also apparent that the gradient is substantially steeper for the older children. In the most affluent neighbourhood, trust is actually higher amongst the oldest children than it is for the youngest. In the most deprived two neighbourhoods, trust is dramatically lower amongst the oldest as opposed to the youngest children. This is not true longitudinal data, so inferences about change with age have to be made cautiously. However, a developmental pattern consistent with the data would be the following: children everywhere start out about equally trusting. As they get older, they obtain more and more experience from the wider environment. For children in affluent neighbourhoods, this experience maintains their trust. In more deprived neighbourhoods, the experiences they have corrode trust, so that the older they are, the less they trust. The greater the deprivation, the greater the rate of corrosion.

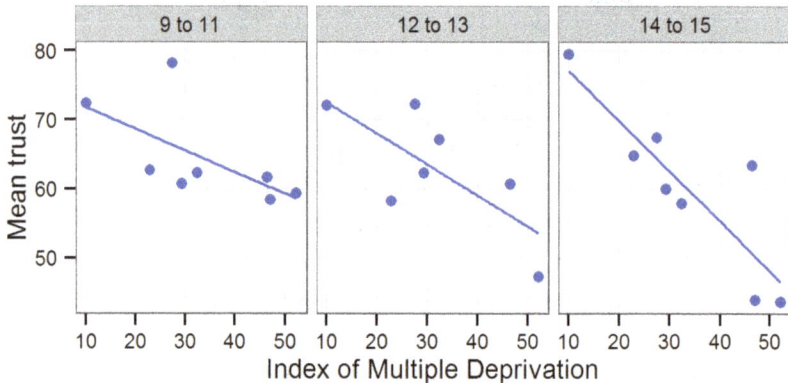

Figure 5.4 Mean trust by neighbourhood deprivation and age group, from the schools survey. Lines represent best fits from regression models. Note that one neighbourhood has no data from the middle age group. Image © Daniel Nettle, CC BY.

The combination of the observational data and the School Survey data suggest, then, that our paradoxical findings regarding social interactions and trust hold true for the lives of young people too. In deprived Tyneside neighbourhoods, it seems that young people have greater social autonomy and greater interaction with neighbours beyond the household, both with members of their own generation and the one above. However, they also feel less able to trust in others, and as they gain more experience of their social world through childhood and into adolescence, the gulf in social trust across the deprivation spectrum continues to get larger.

Social trust through adulthood

The finding from the Schools Survey that, in deprived neighbourhoods, trust is lower in older age groups prompted me to go back to Social Survey 1 to ask the same question of adults. Do the oldest adults trust the least? If social experience under conditions of deprivation cumulatively corrodes trust, then you might imagine that the older you got under such conditions, the less you would trust (think of Edgar at the end of *King Lear*: 'The oldest hath borne most...'). On the other hand, trust may have reached its long-term equilibrium level by early adulthood, which would produce a flat line of trust against age amongst adults.

Figure 5.5 shows the relationship of trust to age by neighbourhood from Social Survey 1. Far from trust being higher in the youngest and lower in the oldest age groups, it is at its highest amongst the over-70s. Trust is positively associated with age in both neighbourhoods, but, as you can see, the slope of the relationship is much steeper in B. It can't be very steep in A because there is nowhere for it to go: even amongst the 20-somethings in A, trust is around 6 on a 7-point scale. By contrast, there is room for an increase with age in B, because many of the men and women in their 20s give trust its lowest possible rating of 1. The pattern of trust against age in Social Survey 2 is much the same. You can also control for how long the respondent has lived in the neighbourhood. Not only is there no relationship between trust and number of years in the neighbourhood, but controlling for duration of residence does not abolish the age pattern.

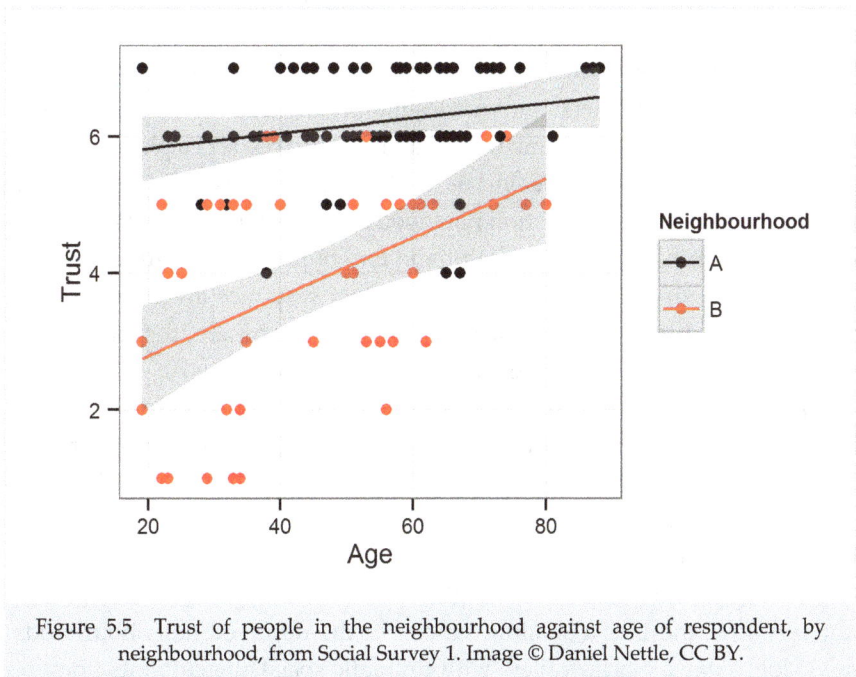

Figure 5.5   Trust of people in the neighbourhood against age of respondent, by neighbourhood, from Social Survey 1. Image © Daniel Nettle, CC BY.

Here we hit the frustration of having only cross-sectional rather than longitudinal data, for there are two different mechanisms that could lie behind the pattern in Figure 5.5 (or it could represent a combination of them). First, there could be a generational difference. Respondents aged 60 and above probably made their way in the world when Neighbourhood B was a less economically uncertain place than it is now, so perhaps the relative security they enjoyed then helped them set up solid social networks and a trusting worldview. The 50–something generation in B shows slightly lower trust: they were making their way 30 years ago, when deindustrialisation was at its height. The group with the lowest trust of all, the 20-somethings, have come into adulthood with industry long gone, opportunities uncertain, dilapidation evident, and demolitions going on all around them. It would be no surprise to find that they are the most socially alienated generation.

This generational hypothesis suggests that the current 20-somethings will carry their low trust with them as they grow older. The alternative hypothesis is a developmental one: perhaps a person's trust changes as they age. Trust has previously been found to increase with age between the ages of 20 and 90 (Twenge, Campbell, & Carter, 2014), whilst studies of related measures of social wellbeing have found U-shaped curves, with levels highest in youth and again in retirement, but with a long dip in the middle (Blanchflower & Oswald, 2008). Perhaps we are seeing something similar here. As children, we are buffered to some extent from negative social interactions, and so our trust tends to be high. We move into the difficult phase of becoming established as independent householders, our worries mount and our trust dips, and then we come through to the autumn of life having found our social place, with our greatest dangers and trials behind us, and so we can relax and trust more. If we attached the high-deprivation neighbourhood data points for 9-11, 12-13, and 14-15 from figure 5.4 to the left-hand end of the Neighbourhood B data points from figure 5.5, we would indeed see a very nice inverted U-shape, with trust very high at the starting age of 9, corroding by age 15, spectacularly low in the 20s, and gradually recovering to be high again by 70.

Whichever mechanism—generational difference or individual change—is driving the pattern in Figure 5.5, there is one thing that seems to be the case: deprivation matters. If there is a generational decline in trust, it has been much worse in the deprived Neighbourhood B and is scarcely perceptible in Neighbourhood A. If there is an individual U-shape curve, then Figures 5.4 and 5.5 suggest that in affluent neighbourhoods the nadir of the U is really not very low: the U is a shallow saucer. In the deprived neighbourhoods, the U looks like a glacial valley, with dramatic social alienation its floor. So whatever the general dynamics, deprivation dramatically exacerbates them. This echoes our findings from chapters 3 and 4 that the social differences between Neighbourhoods A and B are large and basically negative, despite the greater level of social interaction going on there.

No country for old men

What happens to older people in our two neighbourhoods? The Street Ages Dataset gives us some insight into differences in their activities. As you may recall from chapter 2, for this dataset Rebecca and Agathe walked transects of the streets during the school holidays and estimated the ages of all the people they encountered. In Figure 5.6, I have grouped their estimated ages into four categories, under 19, 20-39, 40-59, and 60+, and plotted the percentage of observations from each neighbourhood that falls into each group.

There are a number of things you can do with Figure 5.6. The first is to compare the age distribution of people on the streets from each neighbourhood. What you see is a big excess of the young—under 19 and 20-39—in Neighbourhood B relative to A, and a big deficit in the over-40s and especially the over-60s. The over-60s is the striking one; you only see about half as many in B as in A. It could be that the researchers were not equally good at estimating ages in the two neighbourhoods, but if anything you might expect people in B to age more prematurely, and thus for more people there to be classified as over 60 regardless of actual age. This bias would therefore work in the opposite direction to the pattern we see in the figure. Thus, relative to A, the streets of B are places with an excess of children and young adults, and few visible old people.

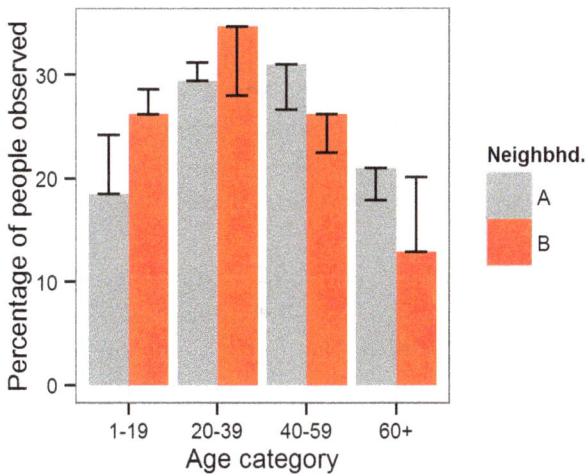

Figure 5.6 The percentage of observations in each neighbourhood by age group, from the Street Ages Dataset. The T-bars connect the observed percentage to the percentage that ought to have been expected given the actual age distribution of residents in the 2001 census. Data described in detail in Nettle, Colléony, and Coyne (2012). Image © Daniel Nettle, CC BY.

The second thing we can do is compare the observed age distribution with what we *ought* to see given who lives there. We have the actual age distribution of residents from the 2001 census. This was some years earlier than our data collection, but let us assume that the age structure has not changed substantially. We can therefore work out a baseline expectation of what we ought to see on the assumption that all age groups have the same tendency to use the streets. This is what is shown by the T-bars on Figure 5.6: each T-bar connects the observed percentage of that age group to the percentage we ought to have expected to see, given the census data.

Children and young people are, perhaps rather surprisingly, under-represented compared to what they should be in both neighbourhoods. The pattern I want to draw attention to, though, is at the other end of the age spectrum. In Neighbourhood A, we should have expected that about 18% of our observations would be 60+. In fact, 21% were. The older people of Neighbourhood A are out in force. In Neighbourhood B, we should have expected 20% to be 60+. In fact, 13% were. The older people of Neighbourhood B have gone missing.

Why is this pattern significant? There are several reasons. For one thing it reminds us that Neighbourhood B is a place where growing older goes badly. Deprived neighbourhoods in England have a slightly lower life expectancy than affluent ones, but the gap in expectation of *healthy* life is vastly greater, amounting to well over a decade (Bajekal, 2005; Nettle, 2010a). In deprived areas, people's health declines more rapidly with age, and they spend more of their adult years prior to death in a state of disability. What we see in the Street Ages Dataset is at least in part the social consequence of this fact. The senior citizens of Neighbourhood A are in good health and use their time to be out and about on the streets. Many of the senior citizens of B are—presumably—indoors, restricted by their health.

The other reason that the pattern is interesting concerns not so much the senior citizens themselves, but the effect of their absence on everyone else. We saw earlier in the that the most trusting social group, with the possible exception of very young children, is the over-60s. This is particularly true in Neighbourhood B. Along with trust go prosocial attitudes, willingness to uphold norms, and so on. This group is over-represented in the street life of A and under-represented in street life of B. In B, their place is taken by an over-representation of the 20-39s in particular. But that group, we can see from Figure 5.5, is the least trusting and, we presume, most suspicious and least prosocial of all the groups we have studied. More generally, crime, antisocial behaviour, and violence are specialities of the young.

This is bound to have an effect on the social ethos of the two places. What would happen if someone collapsed on the streets? If there were misdemeanours or misadventures going on? The answer presumably depends on who was passing by; in A, you've got a much better chance that person will be a trusting 65 year-old lady, and in B, a much better chance she will be an alienated 25 year-old. The very visible absence of the most prosocial age groups may thus contribute, through a number of pathways, to the relative dearth of prosocial behaviour and the relative prevalence of antisocial behaviour in Neighbourhood B. Those pathways include the direct (the lack of the social sanctioning behaviour of older citizens contributes to a failure to inhibit the spread of disorder in public spaces) and the more psychological (the observation that there are mainly young adults on the streets contributes to a feeling of unease and menace). This is another loop with the potential to be self-sustaining: the more threatening the environment feels, the more senior citizens will not want to be out in it, and, with fewer senior citizens, the more threatening it then feels.

The lack of senior citizens on the streets is a source of information in a much more general sense too. When we are young, we are under uncertainty about what kind of future we might have. We can use the older people we see around us in the community—their numbers as well as their state—as a source of information about what the probability distribution of that future might be. On the streets of Neighbourhood A, you see about 71 over-60s for every one hundred people aged 20-39. Most of them look great, too: expensively dressed, vigorous, and moderately likely to be carrying a tennis racket. Simplistically, you might imagine an unconscious mental computation in a 25 year-old that takes input from the surrounding population and says: it looks like if I have made it this far, there is a 71% chance of making it to a good old age in good health. I have lots of time ahead and lots to look forward to.

On the streets of Neighbourhood B, for every one hundred 20-39 year-olds, there are only about 37 over-60s. The same unconscious algorithm would produce a very different output: looking around me, I probably don't have much time. It is less than an even bet that I will be active at 60. The future looks neither bright nor very long.

I have no direct evidence that these particular unconscious mental algorithms exist, but it is a plausible idea. The idea connects the Street Ages Dataset to another aspect of the School Survey. In that survey we asked our young respondents to estimate how long they thought they would live, and also to rate on a scale of 1-100 how optimistic they felt about their futures. The neighbourhood averages by level of deprivation are shown in Figure 5.7. As you can see, the more deprived the neighbourhood, the shorter respondents felt they would live, and the less optimistic about their futures they were. Sadly, they were correct: having been born in more deprived areas, they will live less long, and their futures will be less rosy in myriad other ways too. Their dim perceptions of their futures will in turn help perpetuate the social malaise of the deprived neighbourhoods. A wealth of research shows that a sense of the future as short and unpromising is a key psychological driver of nihilistic behaviours such as self-neglect, taking risks, breaking laws, aggression, and unwillingness to cooperate with others (Brezina, 2009; Caldwell, Wiebe, & Cleveland, 2006; McDade et al., 2011). What interests me is not just the consequences of people perceiving that their lives will be shorter and harder, but also the causes. The (at least partly veridical) idea that life will be relatively short and hard must have got into the minds of the young people in the deprived neighbourhoods somehow. But how? Some of them were only 9 years old. This brings into focus the key issue of psychological mechanisms: how do people turn the psychological inputs they receive (through their life experiences in their communities) into internal representations of how they ought to behave? The next chapter draws together what we have learned about this question.

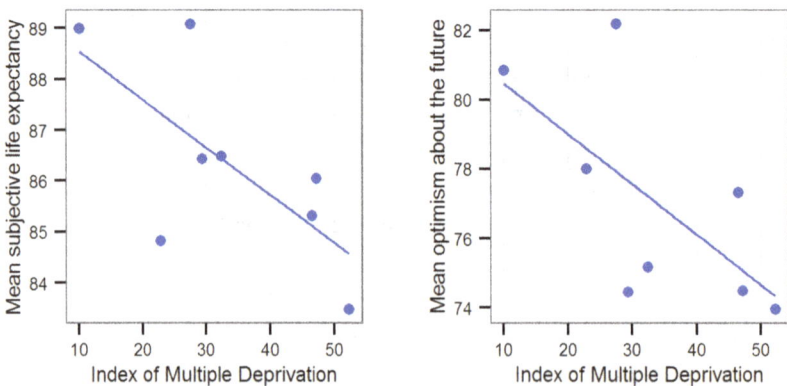

Figure 5.7 Neighbourhood means of subjective life expectancy (years, left panel) and optimism about the future (scale of 1-100, right panel) by Index of Multiple Deprivation. Lines represent best fits from linear regression models. Data from the School Survey. Image © Daniel Nettle, CC BY.

6. Being there

The places you play and where you stay,
Looks like one great big alleyway.

Introduction

As I mentioned in chapter 1, the Tyneside Neighbourhoods Project was not just about how behaviour varies from neighbourhood to neighbourhood, but also about the psychological mechanisms underlying this variation. I hope you will grant me, from all the data presented so far, that social behaviour differs profoundly from Neighbourhood A to B. I hope you will also grant me that a plausible explanation for this is that living in Neighbourhood A affects people in specific ways that are different from the ways living in Neighbourhood B affects the people who live there. That is, I assume that the behavioural differences between A and B are to a considerable extent *consequences* of living in those places, rather than being due some other exogenous factor, such as differential migration of people with certain personalities to certain neighbourhoods.

This raises a fundamental question: how does your psychology come to be affected by the community you live in? The classic anthropological answer invokes acculturation, as if no further elaboration was required: in the words of Herder quoted by Morin (2015), people just absorb their culture like 'a wet sponge that has long been soaking on a wet floor'. The more you examine this metaphor, the more you realise that invoking acculturation without further unpacking does not explain anything. Things outside the mind (acts, artefacts, etc.) cannot literally move inside the mind

 http://dx.doi.org/10.11647/OBP.0084.06

as the water can move into the sponge. The most that can happen is that the mind can construct certain kinds of internal representations (beliefs, memories, attitudes) in a way that is driven by cues in its environment. These cues might—or might not—be there in the local environment because of the behaviour of other members of the community, behaviour that might in turn be driven by the beliefs, memories, and attitudes that *they* hold. Thus, when we say that you can acquire attitude x from others in your community through acculturation, what we mean is that: (1) the attitude x held by others causes them to emit certain classes of environmental cues, (2) these cues can be detected, and (3) these cues increase the probability of your mind constructing x rather than some alternative attitude. This immediately raises more fascinating and more tractable questions. What are the cues? How do we detect them? What timescale do they operate on?

Scholarly discussions of acculturation also tend to overstate the importance of simple imitation, as if cultural traditions were reducible to people copying the acts of others in their surrounding communities. The problem with this is that it does not account for the open-endedness of behaviour; people can come up with appropriate and socially-patterned decisions for situations they have never faced before, and never seen anyone else face either. For example, when participants were asked to play Kari Britt Schroeder's Theft Game (chapter 4), they had never played that game or even been in a closely similar situation before. Thus, there is no way they could have been following a rule of the kind 'behave in this game as I have seen others from my community behave in this game on previous occasions'. Yet they came up with coherent patterns of responses that were systematically different across Neighbourhoods A and B.

Instead, we must assume that they first parsed Kari's game into components that did have analogues in daily life: the concept of opportunistically taking something from someone else; the concept of prosocially standing up for someone else, and so on. Then, to decide on a course of action given these components, they would need to consult a whole set of what are known in the jargon as internal regulatory variables (Tooby, Cosmides, Sell, Lieberman, & Sznycer, 2008). Internal regulatory variables are running mental meters of some aspect of the environment or your own state. For example, social trust is an internal regulatory variable that tells me to what extent the behaviour of others is likely to be benign and reliable. When a stranger asks me for help in some complex way, I evaluate his demand with reference to my level of social trust. If my level of social trust is high, then I am prepared to believe his story and risk helping him; if past experiences have made my level of social trust low, then I will be more sceptical and disinclined to help.

Viewed in this light, the question of how acculturation happens becomes partly the question of how, through our experiences, the levels of our internal regulatory variables are set. They will no doubt be affected by personal interactions (every experience of betrayal, for example, probably brings trust down a notch). They will also be affected by the stories recounted to us by others about their experiences. However, there is also an important role for immediate perceptual input, and it is this role I particularly wish to explore in this chapter.

Perceptual experience and context sensitivity

Every time you go out of your house, you are exposed to a barrage of perceptions: where people are, what they are doing, how they look, the state of their houses, the state of public structures, and so forth. Even if you have no interaction of any consequence with these people and structures, they constitute a rich source of information about what might happen if you *were* suddenly called upon to interact with them. Even the simplest act of visual perception, like recognizing that an object is a teacup, is more than a question of passively receiving photons. It is a process of active inference from the patterns of photons received, in which the mind reconstructs aspects not directly present in the signal, such as the shapes of obscured parts of the objects. I suggest that these inferential processes go well beyond just deciding what kinds of objects are out there, and calibrate the internal regulatory variables governing our social attitudes too. That house has barbed wire on its gate (perception); the people living in it feel at risk from intrusion (inference); I should be careful living in this community (updating of internal regulatory variable). Such updating could happen without any explicit verbal instruction, and without my needing to actually be a victim of violent intrusion myself.

This view of acculturation as involving the setting of internal regulatory variables through perceptually-based inference leads us to ask how long it needs to take. A classical view would be that acculturation takes (and lasts) a lifetime: children are socialized in particular ways, the effects of socialization are gradual and cumulative, and the result is a pattern that, by adulthood, is largely set in stone. There are certainly data that support this view, such as the classic findings that young men socialized in the US Southern states behaved differently from those socialized in the North even when both groups were currently living in the same city and attending the same university (Cohen, Nisbett, Bowdle, & Schwarz, 1996). However, it is unlikely that all internal regulatory variables have to be set in stone. At least some of them remain flexible through life and are constantly being notched up and down by the flow of perception. We can imagine a continuum of cases. At one end would be cases where by adulthood, the amount by which the variable could move up and down from hour to hour with further perceptual experience was very limited. Most of the variation in the variable would therefore be between people with different long-term cultural backgrounds, and the variation within people over time would be negligible. We will call variables at this end of the continuum *trait-like.* The variation in these trait-like variables would still be environmental rather than genetic in origin, but once people were adults there would be little scope for further fluctuation.

At the other end of the continuum would be cases where the variable still had a lot of room to vary in response to changes in the ongoing stream of experience. Put the person in one situation, the variable goes straight up; move them to another situation, it comes straight down. We will call variables at this end of the continuum *contextually sensitive.* Here, most of the variation would be relatable to the person's current situation rather than their longer-term history. This raises the question of whether the psychological differences underlying the different behavioural outcomes between Neighbourhoods A and B are more trait-like or more contextually sensitive. (In Sampson's [2012] terminology, this equates to the question of whether we are dealing with developmental or situational neighbourhood effects.) This question really matters because of its implications for social interventions. If the differences are mainly trait-like, then moving adults from Neighbourhood B to Neighbourhood A would not make them any more trusting; as the saying goes, you can take the woman out of the West End, but not the West End out of the woman. On the other hand, if the differences are mostly contextually sensitive, then moving adults from B to A, or perhaps more relevantly improving the physical environment of B, could have marked real-time effects on trust and other social outcomes.

There is evidence suggesting that many of the internal regulatory variables underlying social behaviour are particularly context-sensitive. Perhaps the strongest comes from Keizer, Lindenberg, and Steg's (2008) experiments. To recall, in their experimental conditions, they sowed the environment with small cues as simple as graffiti on a wall, bicycles parked in violation of a rule or supermarket shopping carts that had not been returned to the proper place. These cues were purely perceptual; they had no direct consequence for the participant. They were also very subtle, but they all suggested in some way or other that people around here were routinely failing to be prosocial. The consequences of the experimental treatments were that the participants started to behave antisocially in lots of other ways, some of them more serious, such as stealing €5. Thus, the participants were not just copying the behaviour implied by the cues, but were using the cues to recalibrate some internal regulatory variable that then affected their decisions in other social domains. Most importantly for current purposes, the effects were dramatic: in real time, through perceptual means alone, the experimenters made the normally prosocial Dutch into a rather antisocial community.

We therefore want to ask whether the differences in social behaviour between the residents of Neighbourhoods A and B reflect context-sensitive responses to immediate experience, or whether they are more trait-like. Some evidence for context-sensitivity comes from the results of Kari's norms experiment in Neighbourhood B, as described in chapter 5. We also carried out another ambitious experiment to try to probe for context-sensitivity, and this is described in the next section.

An experiment with minibuses

An ideal experiment to investigate context-sensitivity would involve taking a group of residents from Neighbourhood A and moving them to Neighbourhood B, directing another group in the opposite direction, and having two control groups that stay where they are. We could then track key psychological variables such as trust over time: to the extent to which trust is context-sensitive, the two moving groups should come to resemble their new neighbours rather than their old ones. How fast the change happened would tell you something about just how labile the context-sensitive variables were. Something slightly akin to this experiment was performed by one of the most ambitious US federal housing programs ever, *Moving to Opportunity*, which provided some poor families with vouchers allowing them to move to more affluent neighbourhoods, whilst some went to other poor neighbourhoods and some stayed where they were. The consequences for the participants' health and behaviour were complex, but, overall, they provide some of the strongest causal evidence we have for the importance of neighbourhood effects (Kessler et al., 2014; Ludwig et al., 2012; Sciandra et al., 2013).

We discussed such an experiment at length within the Tyneside Neighbourhoods Project, and concluded that we did not have a workable way of doing it. However, we did come up with a design for a study that shared some interesting features with such an experiment, but in a much smaller way. This was the work of Gillian Pepper, Kari, and myself, ably assisted by Ruth Jobling and students Bobbie-Jay Hasselby and Anna Wilson. What if, instead of transplanting people from A to B and vice versa, we recruited a third group of adults, residents of neither A or B, and randomly assigned them to spend some time in the environment of one or the other neighbourhood? Let us call these two experimental groups A-visitors and B-visitors. We could then measure some important variables such as trust in both groups. The null hypothesis would be that there should be no systematic differences between them. After all, the two groups were formed by random assignment. If, on the other hand, people are sensitive to neighbourhood context, then the A-visitors should be more highly trusting than the B-visitors, just as residents of A are more trusting than residents of B. The more similar the psychological measures were in A-visitors to A residents, and B-visitors to B residents, the more we would feel it plausible that the differences between residents of A and B were the outcome of immediate responses to context. Of course, we would still be well short of proving that if you moved people from B to A they would soon begin trusting like the other residents of A, but it would nonetheless be an intriguing result.

Two things became clear about this experiment. The first was that we did not want our participants to know about the hypothesis, or even the nature of the study design. It would be too easy for them to offer us the obvious stereotypes about different parts of the city if they knew that was what we were asking about. So the experiment had to be somewhat surreptitious; we had to get our participants into the neighbourhoods on some plausible ulterior motive and then slip our measures in. The second thing that became clear is that our experiment would have to be audaciously short. You can't make people go and spend three weeks in a neighbourhood without really telling them why. It was going to have to be not much more than a quick walk around. This seemed to stack the odds against our finding anything. Our participants' experiences of the neighbourhoods they were assigned to were going to be so small and fleeting that it was hard to believe we would see any measurable effect. However, there is some precedent for very fast-acting effects of exposure to a cultural context. It is well established that, in viewing scenes, Westerners tend to focus most on foreground objects, and

Japanese more on the background and relationships between objects in the scene. What is less well known is that just making American participants view 95 images of Japanese street scenes causes their perceptual style to shift substantially towards a Japanese one, whilst making Japanese participants view images of the US shifts them towards the American style (Miyamoto, Nisbett, & Masuda, 2006). The streets of the USA and Japan just look different. Thus, part of the difference between Americans and Japanese is not so much a matter of long socialization but the way the perceptual system is being driven by its immediate inputs.

For our experimental design, what we settled on in the end was a case of killing two birds with one stone. We were always needing to deliver questionnaires to addresses in Neighbourhoods A and B, as part of the ongoing social surveying. We decided to recruit research volunteers who would help with these deliveries for an hour or two. This involved them showing up at a meeting point in the university, and being randomly shown into one of two minibuses. One minibus would go to Neighbourhood A and one to Neighbourhood B. Each participant would be given a list of addresses, a personalised street map, and a packet of questionnaires. The minibus would wait at a central point and the participant would return to it when they had finished (the 52 participants we recruited ended up taking 10–48 minutes to make their deliveries). As soon as they were back at the minibus, we would measure the psychological variables we were interested in. I found this delivery paradigm promising. When you are trying to find an address to deliver a questionnaire, you really look around you. You see the different streets and types and conditions of housing as you search for the required address; you get lost and have to back up; sometimes you ask a local. In other words, you are for that period alert and richly immersed in and attentive to all the cues about social life that the neighbourhood's streets have to offer.

As for the measures, the idea was to measure in the minibus riders some of the very same things we had responses on from the residents of the two neighbourhoods. We had measures of social trust and personal trust from Social Survey 2 (see chapter 3), so we measured these on the same scale in the minibus riders. We also decided to measure paranoia, the feeling that others intend to do us harm, using a standard questionnaire scale. To get some resident data on paranoia, we recruited an extra 65 householders who got a new Social Survey containing paranoia as well as social and personal trust; it was—with pleasing neatness—these questionnaires that our minibus riders were tasked with delivering.

The results from the minibus study are summarised in Figure 6.1. Each panel represents a different psychological measure. Within each panel, the first pair of bars represents the scores for the residents of the two neighbourhoods, and the second, the scores for the visitors (the resident paranoia scores have been adjusted for age, sex and non-local origin, all factors known to affect paranoia). Taking social trust first, amongst the residents there is the expected neighbourhood difference, with social trust much higher in A than B. What is much more surprising is that difference is mirrored almost perfectly in the minibus riders: visitors to Neighbourhood A rated their social trust higher than those who had visited Neighbourhood B. Moreover, the trust ratings of visitors to Neighbourhood A were not significantly different from those of Neighbourhood A residents, but *were* significantly different from those of Neighbourhood B residents, whilst the ratings of visitors to Neighbourhood B were not significantly different from those of Neighbourhood B residents, but were significantly different from those of Neighbourhood A residents. In other words, minibus riders who had been in neighbourhoods for 10-48 minutes looked exactly like long-term residents of those neighbourhoods. It is important to stress that we did not ask them to imagine how much they thought they would trust if they were a resident of this neighbourhood, or to guess how much the people they had delivered surveys to trusted, or to think about trust right now in particular. We asked them how much they, as a matter of fact, trusted people they met for the first time.

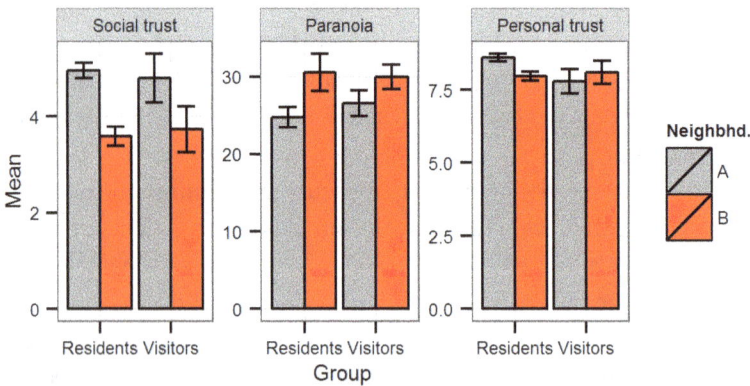

Figure 6.1 Mean social trust (left panel), paranoia (centre panel), and personal trust (right panel) for residents of and visitors to each neighbourhood. Error bars represent one standard error. Data described more fully in Nettle, Pepper, Jobling, and Schroeder (2014). Image © Daniel Nettle, CC BY.

The results for paranoia (centre panel) are rather similar to those for social trust. There is the expected neighbourhood difference amongst the residents, with paranoia higher in Neighbourhood B than A. This pattern is reflected in the minibus riders: visitors to B are more paranoid than visitors to A, and the paranoia scores of visitors to a neighbourhood are statistically indistinguishable from the paranoia scores of the people who live there. Again, the paranoia questionnaire did not ask participants about paranoid thoughts at this moment in particular, or the paranoia they would hypothetically feel if they lived here, but their own self-assessment of their thoughts concerning whether others in general were out to do them harm.

The third trait, personal trust (the trust of people you know well), did not show the same pattern. As already mentioned in chapter 3, there was a neighbourhood difference amongst the residents on this variable. There was no significant difference between the two visitor groups. In a way, though, this is the exception that proves the rule. By putting people into the general social environment of one or other neighbourhood, we had manipulated the informational inputs to regulatory variables concerning what to do in interactions with people they did not know. We had not manipulated any information about the people they did know well, and so we should not have expected effects on internal regulatory variables concerning interactions with known others.

What the results for social trust and paranoia suggest is that key psychological variables that differ between Neighbourhoods A and B are highly sensitive to context, and are notched up and down by recent perceptual experiences of the social environment. Therefore, the results imply, all you have to do to make someone think and feel like a Neighbourhood B resident is make them walk about a mile in the shoes of a Neighbourhood B resident around the streets that a Neighbourhood B resident would see every day. This was for me a stunning finding: I imagined that the low trust and higher paranoia of B residents was the cumulative effect of many years (generations perhaps) of acculturation into a world of economic and social uncertainty. The idea that you could reproduce essentially the *whole* of the Neighbourhood A/B trust difference in a group of experimental volunteers within one hour without doing anything in particular to them, just by having them be there, made me consider the neighbourhood differences in a whole new light. Of course, I am not claiming that *all* of acculturation is a simple matter of immediate context-sensitivity, or that all neighbourhood effects are contextual rather than developmental ones. That is clearly not the case; if I send you to the

Arctic for an hour, you certainly will not become Inuit. However, perhaps the psychological differences we observe between human groups are more a result of sensitivity to immediate perceptual context than we have previously imagined.

The results of this experiment should be relatively encouraging. If the differences between people from deprived neighbourhoods and people from affluent ones were mostly trait-like, then there would be no easy social interventions. Making the West End look cleaner, safer, and better cared for would not be expected to produce immediate gains in terms of greater trust and prosociality: any such gains might be a generation in coming. The experiments by Keizer and colleagues (2008) already suggest that this is not right, and our minibus study seems, in a different way, to confirm the picture. Simply changing the way the environment looks might have substantial impacts on people's internal regulatory variables, and hence, perhaps, their social behaviour. We will return to the potential for such interventions in chapter 7. However, you would not be able to get very far in designing them until you had explored a follow-up question: what is it that people see in Neighbourhood B that lowers their trust and raises their paranoia?

The social diet

Our results, and those of Miyamoto and colleagues (2006) on Japanese-American differences, bring to mind so-called visual diet effects in the perception literature (Rhodes, Jeffery, Watson, Clifford, & Nakayama, 2003; Webster, Kaping, Mizokami, & Duhamel, 2004). Visual diet experiments have shown that you can rapidly alter people's assessment of reality through manipulating their exposure to visual inputs. For example, if you show people a series of slightly angry faces, their view of what a normal neutral face looks like becomes, in a very few minutes, re-centred towards the angry end of the spectrum. Moreover, non-angry faces start to look odd to them. These visual diet effects are found for basic parameters such as size, shape, and proportions as well as socially-laden ones such as facial expression.

Visual diet effects are very strong and very reliable. What is odd about them is that they should exist at all: participants in these experiments have had many years of life experience of what facial expressions normally look like. It is hard to understand why the brain's perceptual mechanisms should be designed to devalue all of that accumulated information about the world and give so much weight to just a few dozen recent exemplars. For whatever reason, though, this is how it seems to work. Internal social regulatory variables such as trust might work in a similar way, and here it is perhaps easier to see why an extreme sensitivity to the most recent inputs might be a good design. People presumably have always moved frequently from social grouping to social grouping. The right level of trust has thus not been something that could be set once and for all, but rather something that constantly needed notching up and down every time to the social context changed. Thus, perceptual mechanisms that scoured the current environment for cues to the right current level would always have been useful.

If basic perceptual regulatory variables like expectations about the shapes of faces are set by the visual diet—the set of recent facial exemplars offered by the environment—then the analogous concept for social regulatory variables like trust is the *social diet*. The social diet is the set of perceptually-available cues about how people in the current context approach social behaviour. Let us think about how the social diet available in Neighbourhood B might differ from that in Neighbourhood A. There are actually a lot of ways in which it will be similar: they are both urban contexts, with buildings of similar vintage, similar numbers of people around, similar vehicles and advertising, similar street signs. However, there are some differences that our data allow us to clearly identify.

A first difference is that the environment of Neighbourhood B contains more cues of prior antisocial behaviour by others, the most striking being litter. In Observational Dataset 1 (chapter 3), we saw someone drop litter every 30 minutes in B as against every 3 hours in A. That is absolutely nothing compared to the difference in litter on the ground. My experience of Neighbourhood B is that litter stays on the ground for many weeks or months, exacerbated by the fact that the system of rubbish collections is not used properly, with many receptacles filled with the wrong materials or at the wrong times, broken, or spilling over. Litter is not the only cue of prior antisocial behaviour, although I believe it to be possibly the most important single one. The iconic broken windows are very much in evidence in Neighbourhood B (Figure 6.2), along with broken bus shelters and other broken structures. It is not uncommon to see evidence of recent fires, presumably deliberately set. These cues say not only 'people round here are prone to behave antisocially', but also, equally importantly, 'no-one round here has been prosocial enough to clear this up', both powerful messages.

Figure 6.2 Empty house in Neighbourhood B. This house sports both broken windows and social defensive measures such as razor wire and steel shutters. Image © Daniel Nettle, CC BY.

A second difference is that Neighbourhood B contains many more cues of social defensive measures (Figure 6.2). Many yard walls in B are topped with razor wire or, particularly brutal looking, broken glass set into concrete. Windows and doors are sometimes protected with thick metal bars. A doctor's surgery on the boundary of B is literally fortified, with anti-climb razors and steel armour on the windows (Figure 6.3). This is almost exactly how police posts looked in Northern Ireland at the height of the Troubles. The irony of these defensive measures is that they are no doubt undertaken with the intention of providing a sense of security. Their effects, however, could be contrary to the intention. Seeing the lengths people round here feel they need to go to to protect themselves powerfully communicates that round here is not a very safe place. Thus, the defensive measures could have the aggregate effect of people in the community ending up feeling, or even perhaps being, less safe than they otherwise would be.

Figure 6.3 Doctor's surgery on the boundary of Neighbourhood B. Defensive measures include a 2m spiked fence, spiked anti-climb rollers, and armoured doors and windows. Image © Daniel Nettle, CC BY.

A third difference in the social diet of the two neighbourhoods concerns police presence and formal law enforcement. The local police, like many police forces, are highly aware of the spatial distribution of incidents requiring their attention, and also concerned with being seen to provide community safety. They patrol Neighbourhood B at a much higher rate than Neighbourhood A. During the gathering of Observational Dataset 1, I was passed by 23 police patrols (mostly in cars; Figure 6.4) in B and 4 patrols in A. Coupled to the patrolling is use of surveillance: much of the West End of Newcastle is fitted with street camera installations (Figure 6.5). The already brutal looking camera towers themselves have to be defended with metal spikes or barbed wire (presumably since, to slightly misuse a bit of Juvenal, nobody is watching the watchmen). No doubt the motivation of the patrols and surveillance is to make people feel safer: if something bad happens to you, we will see it. However, these measures too could have paradoxical effects: if the police have to put that much resource into fighting crime and disorder here, the unconscious inference could go, it must be a *really* bad environment. So it is an open question whether the presence of cues to law-enforcement effort is overall reassuring or alarming.

Figure 6.4 Street scene with police car, Neighbourhood B. Image © Daniel Nettle, CC BY.

Figure 6.5 Surveillance installation amongst houses, Neighbourhood B.
Image © Daniel Nettle, CC BY.

The fourth difference in the social diets between the two neighbourhoods is that already discussed at the end of chapter 5: the relative abundance of older people on the streets of A and their relative scarcity in B. Young adults (especially male ones) are the most dangerous category of human, and moreover the lack of older people might lead to the inference either than this is not a place where life is long, or that this is not a place the frail dare being in the public space. Neither of these inferences would be likely to promote trust or reduce paranoia.

Jessica Hill ran a project to begin to investigate the impact of social diet cues (Hill, Pollet, & Nettle, 2014). She was interested in understanding the effects of two types of cue in particular, cues of disorder and cues of police presence, and also how these two types of cue might interact. By disorder she meant litter, broken windows, neglected buildings and so on. The prior literature was fairly unanimous that people notice and respond to cues of disorder, but very mixed on the subject of visible policing. Some studies had found that it increased feelings of safety, others that it exacerbated the perception of crime risk, and several others that people did not really notice police presence at all. Jessica created three experiments in which participants were exposed to a virtual neighbourhood. In the first experiment the neighbourhood was described verbally, and in the other two it was made using a slide show of real pictures of Neighbourhoods A and B. Each experiment had a factorial design with four conditions. In the first, the virtual neighbourhood featured high disorder and visible police; the second, high disorder and no police; the third, low disorder and visible police; and the fourth, low disorder and no police. Having experienced their virtual neighbourhood, participants were asked to rate it firstly how safe they thought that environment was, and secondly what the social capital of the people who lived there might be (through a series of questions such as whether the people in this neighbourhood could be trusted and whether they were willing to help one another).

The results of the three experiments were remarkably consistent. People responded strongly to cues of disorder, feeling much less safe and perceiving much lower social capital where these cues were present. This is compatible with a wealth of social science research, described above and in earlier chapters, showing that even minor disorder is infectious and prone to undermining social capital and trust. Cues of police presence, by contrast, had no impact whatever in any of the studies. People did not seem to notice them at all. I suppose this has positive implications for the police in that their greatly increased presence in high-crime areas does not seem to exacerbate the fear of crime in those areas. However, it is hardly encouraging if they expected that their visible presence alone would suffice to reduce the fear of crime or bolster the feeling of community trust.

Jessica's study is only a first step, and this part of the Tyneside Neighbourhoods Project represents unfinished business. The kinds of social diet cues we respond to and the kinds of inferences we make from them are topics eminently amenable to experimental investigation. As well as simple slide shows, there are more sophisticated approaches we could use by employing video, eye-tracking, or even immersive virtual reality. These kinds of investigations, as well as being interesting for fundamental reasons, are surely of applied importance, since local governments and agencies have to decide how to allocate their fixed budgets. Surely one of the considerations in such decision-making should be the likely impact of different allocations on citizens' internal regulatory variables such as trust, and hence, on their social behaviour.

7. Conclusions and reflections

But now your eyes sing the sad, sad song,
Of how you lived so fast and died so young.

Introduction

We've now finished the data chapters of this book, and some conclusions are in order. In this chapter, I summarise what strike me as the main things we have learned, and suggest what their implications might be. I then devote a more extended discussion to the issue of causes of patterns of social behaviour, and how our data might bear on it. From this follows a brief consideration of what kinds of interventions we might consider undertaking to try to improve people's wellbeing in deprived neighbourhoods. I end with some further reflection on the ethical difficulties posed by conducting and writing up this research, leading to a modest defence of its value.

Summary and implications of findings

We selected two Tyneside neighbourhoods that were similar in many respects, but fell at opposite ends of the spectrum of socioeconomic deprivation. We used multiple, at times improvised, quantitative methods to try to characterize as best we could the patterns of social behaviour in these two neighbourhoods, and the psychological variables such as trust that underlay them. I set out our enquiries within the framework of two broad narratives: the Kropotkinian view, that harshness and deprivation bring social cooperation to the fore, and the Mountain People view, that

http://dx.doi.org/10.11647/OBP.0084.07

harshness and deprivation corrode cooperation and promote antisocial behaviour.

There was some evidence for greater sociality in the deprived Neighbourhood B: people there socialized more on the streets; were less likely to be alone; greeted one another more as they moved around the neighbourhood; and their children were more likely to be found in multi-household groups. These behavioural observations bring to mind Young and Willmott's (1957) portrayal of working-class community life in East London, and are readily viewed through a Kropotkinian lens. However, most of the other findings, including all of those based on private responses to surveys, suggest the opposite view. When we gave people the opportunity to cooperate with another resident in a monetary game, residents of Neighbourhood B were averse to doing so, even if they could choose the beneficiary themselves. Moreover, when we gave them the chance to steal from other residents, they did so to a much greater extent than the residents of Neighbourhood A. In the same game, they were also less likely to come to the aid of an innocent victim of theft. We observed more littering in Neighbourhood B than A, and letters lost in Neighbourhood B were much less likely to find their way home. Crime and antisocial behaviour was much more frequent, despite vastly greater police effort. All in all, it is hard not to see the bulk of the neighbourhood differences as supporting the view that deprivation corrodes the basis of prosociality and is a fomenting ground for antisocial behaviour.

Underlying the differences in behaviour between the two neighbourhoods lay marked differences in the psychological variables that regulate expectations in social interactions. Residents of Neighbourhood B trusted each other much less than those of A; this included both strangers and people they knew well. The low trust was particularly striking in young adults. Respondents from Neighbourhood B also reported greater feelings of paranoia. They perceived social cheating by others in their neighbourhood to be much more widespread than respondents in A did. Data from children in other parts of Tyneside showed that the association of deprivation and low trust is not restricted to Neighbourhoods A and B, and suggested that as children grow up, trust declines steeply if they live in a deprived neighbourhood, but remains high if they live in an affluent one. It is hard not to see an echo of Turnbull's (1972) claim that under severe deprivation, mistrust and fear become the predominant interpersonal attitudes. These attitudes matter for behaviour: our data suggest that unwillingness to cooperate with others was strongly related to lack of trust, and propensity to take from others was associated with the perception that others in the neighbourhood were cheating anyway. In other words, a kind of golden rule drove people's social decisions: don't cooperate if you don't think others can be trusted to also do so, and get away with as much cheating as you can if you think others are doing likewise.

It would be tempting to explain our findings in terms of the folk-sociological idea that working-class communities based on heavy industries traditionally had high social capital and cohesiveness, and the loss of these industries in the last forty years or so led to the social fragmentation we see today. However, the truth is that we simply don't have the historical data you would need to establish that the golden age was ever really very golden. We have already seen that the suspicion of romanticisation hangs over some past accounts of working-class life. Thus, the best we can say is that social capital is low and social disorder high in our more deprived study site today. We must remain somewhat agnostic about whether this situation is a product solely of deindustrialisation or in fact represents continuity with earlier historical periods; economic conditions were hardly benign for working-class people in pre-deindustrialisation Newcastle, after all.

We tried to address the question of whether the differences in social attitudes between the two neighbourhoods were set in stone by years of acculturation, or represented a more immediate response to context. Our minibus experiment (chapter 6) suggested that low trust and high paranoia might represent an immediate response to being in an environment full of visual cues of disorder. This is consistent with recent work on the spreading of disorder, and the 'broken windows' theory of crime. The minibus findings are perhaps the most intriguing and potentially useful of the whole project, not least since they suggest avenues for intervention, such as a thorough neighbourhood clean-up, that could be relatively quick wins.

It feels odd to end an ethnographic study by talking about possible interventions to 'improve' the social life of my study site. As a social researcher, I naturally start from the principle that social life is neither better nor worse in either of my study populations, just differently organized. To problematize Neighbourhood B as somewhere that needs fixing strikes against this neutral stance, and, as I will argue later in the chapter, presents an ethical risk. However, there are times when the strongest professional imperative is to come off the fence, and this is one of them: social life is, in some important senses, worse for the residents of Neighbourhood B than for those of A. I think we can agree that is worse to feel paranoid than to feel secure, and it is worse to feel you have insufficient social support than to feel you have it in abundance.

What is my justification for these evaluative statements? First and foremost, it is what our participants tell us. In Social Survey 1, we asked respondents how much they liked the neighbourhood. The data are plotted in Figure 7.1. As you can see, almost everyone from Neighbourhood A rated their neighbourhood as a 6 or 7 on a scale where 7 was the maximum. (To be precise, 77% of participants gave it a 7, and exactly one person gave it a score lower than 6.) By contrast, in Neighbourhood B, there is a much greater spread of opinions, and many more low ratings. The median is still 5, which is above the mid-point of the scale, but the difference from the distribution of ratings in Neighbourhood A is very marked. Moreover, the less the individual trusted others in the neighbourhood, the less they liked the neighbourhood. Thus, the residents themselves are telling us that there are things they would prefer to be different.

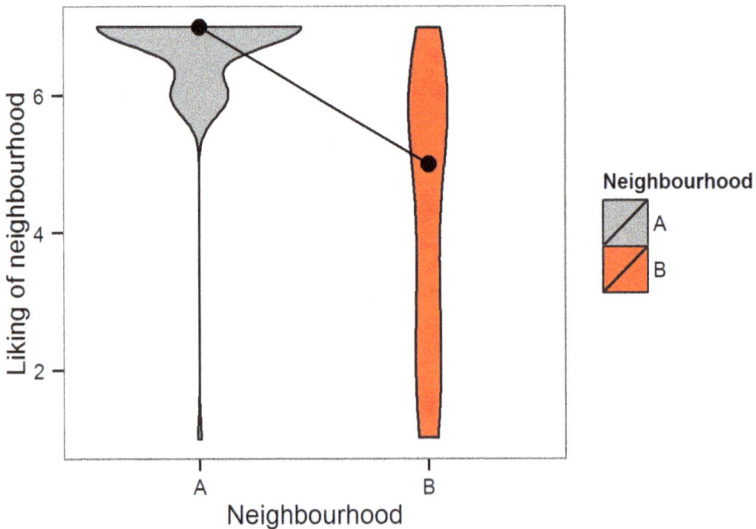

Figure 7.1 Violin plot of respondent ratings of how much they like their neighbourhood, on a scale of 1-7. The black dot shows the median for each neighbourhood. The curved shape represents the distribution of the data on an arbitrary horizontal scale; where the shape is wide, there are many observations, and where it is narrow, there are few. Data from Social Survey 1. Image © Daniel Nettle, CC BY.

A related point is that Neighbourhood B is not a healthy place. At the 2001 census, only 57% of people there described themselves as being in good health, and fully a third of adults of working age reported that they had a limiting long-standing illness. Expectancy of healthy life is a good decade shorter than in affluent areas, and we saw in chapter 5 how there is a dearth of active senior citizens on the streets. We haven't measured it directly, but if Neighbourhood B is like other deprived areas of the UK, then there will be an excess of depression, anxiety, and stress-related illness (Stansfeld & Head, 1998). I can't demonstrate that the poor health in Neighbourhood B is *caused* by the low trust and low social capital; the causality could be the other way around, or both could be separate consequences of something else. However, there are plenty of suggestions in the literature that social capital affects health (Kawachi, Kennedy, & Glass, 1999), and it would be hard to argue that the low social capital and low social trust in Neighbourhood B have any positive benefits. Thus, it does seem justified to ask: how might social wellbeing be made—by the residents' own lights— better in the deprived parts of Tyneside?

The economic grit and the cultural pearl

The issue of possible solutions is inexorably bound up with the issue of causes, which is why it always strikes me as odd when applied researchers display indifference to fundamental explanatory theories; in general terms, how you think you might change a situation should follow from your theoretical understanding of the factors that brought it about. We could privilege economic factors in our account of the causes of the social woes of Neighbourhood B and places like it. The economic deprivation and uncertainty of life in that neighbourhood drive people to short-term self-preservation choices; low social capital and antisocial behaviour must follow. This recalls the Marxist view that the economic base determines the social superstructure, and it also foregrounds the agentic aspect of human nature: people respond to their environments with shifts in their social decisions. On the other hand, we could privilege cultural processes in our account: low social trust and antisocial behaviour are traditions that exist in communities like B. They are passed from person to person through acculturation and have their own replicatory dynamic that is at least somewhat self-sustaining. This account foregrounds the cultural aspect of human nature. In this section, I will try to sketch a view of the probable causes of the social problems of Neighbourhood B that gives weight to both economic and cultural factors. Hence, by implication, I am trying to do justice to both the agentic and cultural aspects of human nature in an integrative explanation of the causes of variation in social behaviour.

Perhaps the most diagnostic difference between economic and cultural accounts of causes concerns the mapping between material situations and social results. Under a strong economic determinism, if you put twenty different human populations into the same set of economic circumstances, you would always get the same result. Economic circumstances X should always produce behaviour pattern Y, and in comparative work, the associations between economic factors and social consequences should be highly consistent. Under the strongest cultural approach, you could put twenty different populations into the same economic situation, and you could get completely different social results each time. What happened would depend on the cultural repertoire that each group started with, and would have plenty of scope to drift off in a different direction each time through the intrinsic dynamics of cultural replication. In the case of deprivation and social behaviour, a strongly economic approach would expect consistent effects of deprivation across multiple populations, whereas a strongly cultural approach would expect that the consequences of deprivation would be different in every case.

The Tyneside Neighbourhoods Project is poorly designed to adjudicate this question, because it did not have twenty different populations all subjected to economic deprivation. It really had only one. Thus, we can't say, on the basis of our data alone, that deprivation always has the effects of lowering trust and raising paranoia. Low trust and high paranoia could be an idiosyncratic cultural trait of Neighbourhood B that would not be replicated in other deprived communities. However, there are many reasons for thinking this is not the case. First, we did have some data from other Tyneside neighbourhoods, via the School Survey, and these data suggested that greater deprivation is reliably associated with lower trust across the conurbation. Second, I am impressed by Haushofer's (2013) findings, which use the World Values Survey and demonstrate that, across 43 countries, every step down the income scale is associated with a measurable diminution of trust. There were no countries where the gradient ran in the other direction. Third, our findings of greater petty crime, increased interpersonal conflict, and greater squalor in the public space, can be found time and time again in ethnographic descriptions of communities facing severe economic hardship, from many different countries, and many different historical periods.

Fourth, and perhaps most importantly, there is the occasional natural experiment we can turn to. My favourite comes from eleven counties of North Carolina, USA (Costello, Compton, Keller, & Angold, 2003). In these counties, antisocial behaviour (basically aggression, violence, and minor law-breaking) was markedly more common amongst children from poor families than those from middle-class families. Many of the poor families were Native Americans. Halfway through the study period, a casino opened on the reservation belonging to the Cherokee. Native American reservations are outside of state laws and so able to host lucrative gambling facilities. As part of the agreement to host the casino, every Cherokee family started to receive a 6-monthly share of the profits, lifting them out of poverty. Within four years of the casino opening, the rates of antisocial behaviour in the previously poor Cherokee families looked exactly the same as the rates in families that had always been middle-class. It did not take generations of slow, gradual evolution for the antisocial culture of these families to disappear: it happened in near-real time as soon as their material difficulties were alleviated. Poor families that did not receive a casino income retained their high levels of antisocial behaviour. This argues for a repeatable and direct causal nexus linking economic factors-poverty and deprivation-to antisocial behaviour.

Let us put this together with the edge principle I adumbrated in chapter 3. There I argued that when people are at the very edge of desperation, they are liable to flip into a short-termist state where they can allocate little or no energy to the social needs of others, and are prepared to risk doing others harm if it furthers their immediate interest to do so. I proposed this as a universal reaction underlain, presumably, by specific psychological mechanisms whose function is to provide some chance of getting through a situation of existential crisis. I did not claim that all of the residents of Neighbourhood B were in this state all of time. Probably the vast majority of them are in it none of the time, and the remainder only very occasionally. However, the probability of such a state being entered is increased by every increment you move down the scale of relative poverty and deprivation. This alone would be sufficient to account, for example, for the results of the Cherokee casino study.

So far, this is a strongly economic account. However, it is not yet complete. What we observed in Neighbourhood B was not just the odd desperate individual performing the odd rash act, but generally low levels of prosociality in the economic games. Here's where cultural processes come in. Cultural processes are, broadly speaking, processes by which people influence other people. They act as spreaders and amplifiers of individual poverty-driven decisions. For example, imagine that someone in a neighbourhood performs one violent and desperate act. Those that witness it notch down their trust as a result. With lower trust, those people are less inclined to participate in keeping the streets around their houses clean. Others see this and lower *their* trust too. There start to be small signs of disorder in the neighbourhood. People see this and internalize it as normative. They feel like they can get away with small vandalisms or thefts. These acts in turn leave signs in the environment to which others respond, and so on. The initial isolated antisocial act leads to cycles of sociocultural ramification that end up with the whole neighbourhood having a very different social equilibrium than it would have done without that act. Social mistrust and social cheating are particularly potent raw materials for cultural processes. This is because each has the potential for feed-forward loops: when one person starts to do it, it produces cues that cause others also to do it more, and this in turn can feed back to the originating person. Thus, cultural forces can take small and sporadic behavioural differences between two neighbourhoods, and turn them into a persistently and pervasively different social ethos.

An apposite metaphor here is that of the grit and the pearl. Pearls start out when a small external irritant enters the shell of a mollusc. Processes intrinsic to the mollusc—repeated secretion of layers of calcium carbonate and conchiolin—then work to build up this stimulus into a much larger pearl. A pearl is much more substantial than the grit it started from, and its detailed shape would not be predictable from the shape of its gritty centre. (Its value and beauty are also greater, but that is irrelevant to the way I am using the metaphor here.) On the other hand, pearls don't get going without the introgression of some grit. I feel much the same about socioeconomic deprivation and antisocial behaviour. If people are materially in a sufficiently bad situation, there will be a high enough rate of desperate incidents to kick-start the cultural evolution process that will very often spiral towards a low-trust, disordered community equilibrium. On the other hand, if people can feel secure that their material needs are dealt with, then the desperate incidents will tend to be so rare that the cultural pearl is relatively unlikely to get going. I am enough of a materialist to assign a causal primacy to the economic base: it is the grit at the heart of the pearl. On the other hand, I would not diminish the role of cultural transmission in amplifying and perpetuating the grit's effects.

Structural change versus nudges

The distinction between the economic grit and the cultural pearl leads us to a distinction between different policy approaches to social problems. On the one hand, you might feel that any attempt to improve the social lot of neighbourhood B needs to be *structural*: it needs to address the fundamental issue that the residents there face poor and uncertain economic prospects. This corresponds to the view that the economic issues are the primary ones. Set against this, there has been a lot of recent interest in purely behavioural or *nudge* interventions (Dolan et al., 2012; Thaler & Sunstein, 2008). The idea of these nudge interventions is that you can have a big effect on outcomes by making small tweaks to the psychological inputs people receive. You can, for example, get people to reduce their electricity consumption by telling them on their bill how much more than neighbouring households they have used. In the domain of social behaviour, many of the possible nudges relate to the cultural amplifying forces discussed in the previous section. You might find ways for residents to communicate to one another all the things they liked about the neighbourhood. A bit more ambitiously, you might clean up all the litter and repair all the broken windows. By thus changing residents' social diets, you would potentially interrupt the self-perpetuating transmission cycle of low trust and opportunistic antisociality.

There is plenty of evidence that nudge-style interventions can work, at least in some populations for some kinds of problem. Findings concerning the spreading of disorder, including our own minibus study described in chapter 6, suggest that the payoffs to simple visible improvements in the social environment of Neighbourhood B could be rapid and quite large. Whilst I can see the value of this, I remain uneasy about the nudge approach as a general solution. It has proved popular with politicians, because it is ostensibly apolitical and hard for anyone to object to. It does not call for any major reform of how our economic system works. We have to ask, though, if the fundamental structural issues are not solved, how long will the gains last? How long before someone who is materially desperate and close to the edge breaks a few windows and the whole cycle starts again? Whilst it may be desirable to arrest the processes that turn grit into pearls, if there is constant stream of new grit, you risk failing to get to the heart of the problem.

The West End of Newcastle has seen a whole series of well-intentioned superficial regeneration schemes. They look nice for a while—and do seem to have medium-term effects on wellbeing (Blackman, Harvey, Lawrence, & Simon, 2001)—but they eventually deteriorate, and as we have seen, the residents of those regenerated areas are still relatively mistrustful and paranoid. By contrast, areas like Neighbourhood A don't receive any expensive makeover schemes and don't need them: those more prosperous communities manage to create and maintain the social ethos they want without any nudging or other anti-entropic external input. And we have already seen the evidence from the Cherokee casino study suggesting that if you can—somehow—fix the structural economic issues, the downstream social problems simply sort themselves out. I find this very striking.

The response I get from my colleagues in the behavioural sciences at this point goes something like this: you need to do both. The nudges may not be a panacea, but they are certainly a help, and they are also something we can get on with doing immediately whilst figuring out how to address the much more knotty long-term structural issues like low incomes, low human capital and insecurity of employment. This is a reasonable position, but there are two possible problems with it. First, when you focus on the easy stuff first, you tend not to ever get around to addressing the hard stuff at all. The hard stuff gets political, reasonable people can disagree over it, and it may require change to our current institutions. Devoting effort to non-structural interventions effectively puts the structural issues out in the long grass.

The second problem is that resources are finite. Money spent on nudges and similar schemes is taken from something else. What might the something else be that would make a greater difference to the social life of poor communities? This question takes us far beyond the data of the present study. However, let me mention a personal view that we should not underestimate the importance of just raising poor people's incomes. There seems to be a widespread perception that the social problems of chaotic lives, public disorder, and antisocial behaviour are somehow not economic: they are not caused by lack of money, and hence more money alone is not the solution to them. We do not actually know that this perception is right. The admittedly limited evidence suggests that raising poor people's incomes improves social and psychological outcomes quite a lot, especially if people can thereby have greater control and security in their lives (in my terms, stop coming or fearing coming close to the edge). There is the Cherokee casino study I have already mentioned, and there are various experiments with minimum incomes policies or negative income taxes (Forget, 2011). These policies appear to have substantial positive impacts on a wide range of fronts. This means that the relevant cost-benefit calculation for any social policy scheme is not: does it have a positive impact? Rather, the question is: does it have a *greater long-term* positive impact than using the same money to raise the guaranteed incomes of people in the most deprived communities?

Just as I tend to accord somewhat of a primacy to the economic grit over the cultural pearl, I would accord rather greater priority to tackling the structural economic issues than to other ways of addressing the social problems of deprived Tyneside neighbourhoods. The elephant in the room is the vast gulf in economic prospects for the kinds of people who live in Neighbourhood B compared to the kinds who live in Neighbourhood A. The concern to tackle the elephant head-on, having become unfashionable for a while, is being discussed by more and more people as the scale and social costs of current levels of economic inequality become clearer. It is not, or should not be, the exclusive preserve of the political left. People of all political persuasions should be able to agree that there is currently a problem. How you propose to tackle the problem will obviously depend on your predelictions. What is clear is that our present mix of institutions—state *and* private-sector—is not doing a good job for localities like Neighbourhood B. Inequality is increasing, and the gulf in social, health, and economic outcomes is widening. We need different institutions, institutions that give ordinary people greater security and control over their lives.

The ethics of representation and the value of ethnography

The interests of deprived localities are not well represented in national discourse: people in those localities are subjected to derision, alarmism, or romanticisation rather than being recognized as normal citizens who have heterogeneous but particular experiences. This leads me to the issue of the ethics of representation, which I foreshadowed briefly in chapter 2. One of the central ideas in this book is to do with the cultural self-perpetuation of social problems. The perception that others are not trusting and do not help spreads from person to person through the cues they leave in the environment. Those cues are not just in the broken windows and litter on the streets. They are also in media articles, television programmes, and, if anybody reads them, academic books. The way I have described social life in Neighbourhood B here may be justified by the data, but it nonetheless risks contributing to the perpetuation of a negative social reputation, and hence of the very outcomes it represents. This has been a source of considerable personal struggle for me, as a committed citizen of the West End of Newcastle, as well as, I hope, an ethical professional researcher. The West End has had enough adversity and bad press; the last thing it needs, it would seem, is to be negatively represented by me.

There is a temptation to allow what one wants to be the case to drive the way one describes what is in fact the case. We saw in Kari's perceived norms experiment (chapter 4) that manipulating the information residents got about what other people thought of their neighbourhood seemed to have an immediate positive impact on their social expectations. If I had carefully and selectively written my book so as to accentuate the positive, it could perhaps itself have become a kind of experimental intervention along those lines, and could have made a small contribution to improving the social ethos of Neighbourhood B. However, my considered judgement is that this would have been an even greater wrong. The primary ethical imperative for an ethnographer is to bear witness to what is the case, without obfuscation. Bearing true witness—and contributing to the understanding of human nature—is likely to do my fellow citizens and their communities more good in the very long term than parochial advocacy or romanticisation. What I present here is information to be fed into the machines of human knowledge and of civil society, with results I cannot entirely predict. I fervently hope that it might eventually do some good. I can only apologise to our participants that it hasn't led to anything concretely or immediately beneficial, which, in all honesty, it hasn't.

If the findings of the Tyneside Neighbourhoods Project make uncomfortable reading at times, I consider this a judgement not on the residents of Neighbourhood B, but on a political and economic system that continues to make the lives of the poorer half of society uncertain and insecure, despite historically unprecedented material abundance. In Selina Todd's words: 'We don't need working-class people to be revolutionary heroes or helpful neighbours in order to make the point that inequality is damaging and wrong' (Todd, 2014). I would go further. If people in the most deprived communities are not helpful neighbours, that can be taken as *evidence* for the proposition that inequality is damaging and wrong. If we continue to make the prosperity and security gap between the favoured few and the rest of society widen as it has done in recent decades, then there will be lower trust, greater paranoia, less help, and more harm for more and more people. That is an issue we all have to think about: political decisions, not laws of nature, determine levels of inequality. And in case you feel after reading this that people from deprived communities are somehow 'other', then you should not. My hunch is that the only important thing differentiating people from Neighbourhood B from people from Neighbourhood A is that they live in Neighbourhood B and face the material problems that Neighbourhood B faces, whereas the people from Neighbourhood A don't. It is only a short bike ride from one to the other.

References

Adams, J., & White, M. (2009). Time perspective in socioeconomic inequalities in smoking and body mass index. *Health Psychology, 28*, 83–90. http://doi.org/10.1037/0278-6133.28.1.83

Adler, N., Boyce, T., & Chesney, M. (1994). Socioeconomic status and health. The Challenge of the gradient. *American Psychologist, 49*, 15–24.

Bajekal, M. (2005). Healthy life expectancy by area deprivation: Magnitude and trends in England, 1994–1999. *Health Statistics Quarterly, 25*, 18–27.

Bardsley, N. (2007). Dictator game giving: Altruism or artefact? *Experimental Economics, 11*, 122–133. http://doi.org/10.1007/s10683-007-9172-2

Baumeister, R. F., Vohs, K. D., & Funder, D. C. (2007). Psychology as the science of self-reports and finger movements: Whatever happened to actual behavior? *Perspectives on Psychological Science, 2*, 396–403. http://doi.org/10.1111/j.1745-6916.2007.00051.x

Beidelman, T. O. (1973). Review of 'The Mountain People.' *Africa, 43*, 170–171.

Bell, A. V., Richerson, P. J., & McElreath, R. (2009). Culture rather than genes provides greater scope for the evolution of large-scale human prosociality. *Proceedings of the National Academy of Sciences of the United States of America, 106*, 17671–17674. http://doi.org/10.1073/pnas.0903232106

Bernasco, W., & Nieuwbeerta, P. (2005). How do residential burglars select target areas?: A new approach to the analysis of criminal location choice. *British Journal of Criminology, 45*, 296–315. http://doi.org/10.1093/bjc/azh070

Blackman, T., Harvey, J., Lawrence, M., & Simon, A. (2001). Neighbourhood renewal and health: Evidence from a local case study. *Health & Place, 7*, 93–103. http://doi.org/10.1016/S1353-8292(01)00003-X

Blanchflower, D. G., & Oswald, A. J. (2008). Is well-being U-shaped over the life cycle? *Social Science and Medicine, 66*, 1733–1749. http://doi.org/10.1016/j.socscimed.2008.01.030

Bourke, A. F. (2011). *Principles of Social Evolution*. Oxford: Oxford University Press.

Brezina, T. (2009). 'Might not be a tomorrow': A multi-method approach to anticipated early death and youth crime. *Criminology, 47,* 1091–1129.

Burton-Chellew, M. N., & West, S. A. (2013). Prosocial preferences do not explain human cooperation in public-goods games. *Proceedings of the National Academy of Sciences of the United States of America, 110,* 216–21. http://doi.org/10.1073/pnas.1210960110

Byrne, D. (1989). *Beyond The Inner City.* Milton Keynes: Open University Press.

Caldwell, R. M., Wiebe, R. P., & Cleveland, H. H. (2006). The influence of future certainty and contextual factors on delinquent behavior and school adjustment among African American adolescents. *Journal of Youth and Adolescence, 35,* 591–602. http://doi.org/10.1007/s10964-006-9031-z

Carpenter, J., Verhoogen, E., & Burks, S. (2005). The effect of stakes in distribution experiments. *Economics Letters, 86,* 393–398. http://doi.org/10.1016/j.econlet.2004.08.007

Cialdini, R. B., Reno, R. R., & Kallgren, C. A. (1990). A focus theory of normative conduct: Recycling the concept of norms to reduce littering in public places. *Journal of Personality and Social Psychology, 58,* 1015–1026.

Cohen, D., Nisbett, R. E., Bowdle, B. F., & Schwarz, N. (1996). Insult, aggression, and the southern culture of honor: An 'experimental ethnography'. *Journal of Personality and Social Psychology, 70,* 945–959. http://doi.org/10.1037/0022-3514.70.5.945

Cornwell, J. (1984). *Hard-Earned Lives: Accounts of Health and Illness from East London.* London: Routledge & Kegan Paul.

Costello, E. J., Compton, S. N., Keller, M., & Angold, A. (2003). Relationships between poverty and psychopathology: A natural experiment. *Journal of the American Medical Association, 290,* 2023–2029.

Côté, S., Piff, P. K., & Willer, R. (2013). For whom do the ends justify the means? Social class and utilitarian moral judgment. *Journal of Personality and Social Psychology, 104,* 490–503. http://doi.org/10.1037/a0030931

Cronk, L., & Wasielewski, H. (2008). An unfamiliar social norm rapidly produces framing effects in an economic game. *Journal of Evolutionary Psychology, 6,* 283–308.

Crow, G., & Allan, G. (1994). *Community Life: An Introduction to Local Social Relations.* Hemel Hempstead: Harvester Wheatsheaf.

Day, G. (2006). *Community and Everyday Life.* Abingdon: Routledge.

Dietz, T., Stern, P. C., & Guagnano, G. A. (1998). Social structural and social psychological bases of environmental concern. *Environment and Behavior, 30,* 450–71.

Dolan, P., Hallsworth, M., Halpern, D., King, D., Metcalfe, R., & Vlaev, I. (2012). Influencing behaviour: The mindspace way. *Journal of Economic Psychology, 33,* 264–277. http://doi.org/10.1016/j.joep.2011.10.009

Dunbar, R. I. M., & Spoors, M. (1995). Social networks, support cliques, and kinship. *Human Nature, 6,* 273–290. http://doi.org/10.1007/BF02734142

Efferson, C., Takezawa, M., & McElreath, R. (2007). New Methods in Quantitative Ethnography. *Current Anthropology, 48,* 912–919. http://doi.org/10.1086/523016

Fehr, E., & Gachter, S. (2000). Cooperation and punishment in public goods experiments. *The American Economic Review, 90,* 980–994.

Forget, E. L. (2011). The Town with No Poverty: The Health Effects of a Canadian Guaranteed Annual Income Field Experiment. *Canadian Public Policy, 37,* 283–305.

Forsythe, R., Horowitz, J., Savin, N., & Sefton, M. (1994). Fairness in simple bargaining experiments. *Games and Economic Behavior, 6,* 347–369. http://doi.org/10.1006/game.1994.1021

Frankenhuis, W. E., & Panchanathan, K. (2011). Balancing sampling and specialization: An adaptationist model of incremental development. *Proceedings Of The Royal Society B-Biological Sciences, 278,* 3558–3565. http://doi.org/10.1098/rspb.2011.0055

Furr, R. M. (2009). Personality psychology as a truly behavioural science. *European Journal of Personality, 23,* 369–401.

George, P. A., & Hole, G. J. (1995). Factors influencing the accuracy of age estimates of unfamiliar faces. *Perception, 24,* 1059–1073.

Grosjean, P. (2014). A history of violence: The culture of honor and homicide in the US South. *Journal of the European Economic Association, 12,* 1285–1316.

Haley, K. J., & Fessler, D. M. T. (2005). Nobody's watching? Subtle cues affect generosity in an anonymous economic game. *Evolution and Human Behavior, 26,* 245–256. http://doi.org/10.1016/j.evolhumbehav.2005.01.002

Halpern, D. (2005). *Social Capital.* Cambridge: Polity Press.

Hamilton, W. D. (1964). The genetical evolution of social behaviour I, II. *Journal of Theoretical Biology, 7,* 1–52.

Haushofer, J. (2013). *The Psychology of Poverty: Evidence from 43 Countries.* Retrieved from http://www.princeton.edu/~joha/

Heine, B. (1985). The Mountain People: Some Notes on the Ik of North-Eastern Uganda. *Africa, 55,* 3–16.

Henrich, J., Boyd, R., Bowles, S., Camerer, C., Fehr, E., Gintis, H., et al. (2005). 'Economic man' in cross-cultural perspective: Behavioral experiments in 15 small-scale societies. *Behavioral and Brain Sciences, 28,* 795–815. http://doi.org/10.1017/S0140525X05000142

Henrich, J., Boyd, R., McElreath, R., Gurven, M., Richerson, P. J., Ensminger, J., et al. (2012). Culture does account for variation in game behavior. *Proceedings of the National Academy of Sciences of the United States of America, 109,* E32–33. http://doi.org/10.1073/pnas.1118607109

Henrich, J., Ensminger, J., McElreath, R., & Barr, A. (2010). Markets, religion, community size, and the evolution of fairness and punishment. *Science, 327,* 1480–1484.

Herrmann, B., Thöni, C., & Gächter, S. (2008). Antisocial punishment across societies. *Science, 319,* 1362–1368.

Hill, J., Jobling, R., Pollet, T. V., & Nettle, D. (2014). Social capital across urban neighborhoods: A comparison of self-report and observational data. *Evolutionary Behavioral Sciences, 8,* 59–69. http://doi.org/10.1037/h0099131

Hill, J., Pollet, T. V., & Nettle, D. (2014). Disorder affects judgements about a neighbourhood: Police presence does not. *PeerJ, 2,* e287. http://doi.org/10.7717/peerj.287

Hill, R. A., & Dunbar, R. I. M. (2003). Social network size in humans. *Human Nature-an Interdisciplinary Biosocial Perspective, 14,* 53–72. http://doi.org/10.1007/s12110-003-1016-y

Holme, A. (1985). *Housing and Young Families in East London.* London: Routledge & Kegan Paul.

Kacelnik, A., & Bateson, M. (1996). Risky theories - The effects of variance on foraging decisions. *American Zoologist, 36,* 402–434. http://doi.org/10.1093/icb/36.4.402

Kacelnik, A., & El Mouden, C. (2013). Triumphs and trials of the risk paradigm. *Animal Behaviour, 86,* 1117–1129. http://doi.org/10.1016/j.anbehav.2013.09.034

Kawachi, I., Kennedy, B. P., & Glass, R. (1999). Social capital and self-reported health: A contextual analysis. *American Journal of Public Health, 89,* 1187–1193. http://doi.org/10.2105/AJPH.89.8.1187

Keizer, K., Lindenberg, S., & Steg, L. (2008). The spreading of disorder. *Science,* 1681–1685.

Keizer, K., Lindenberg, S., & Steg, L. (2013). The importance of demonstratively restoring order. *PloS One, 8,* e65137. http://doi.org/10.1371/journal.pone.0065137

Kessler, R. C., Duncan, G. J., Gennetian, L. A., Katz, L. F., Kling, J. R., Sampson, N. A, et al. (2014). Associations of Housing Mobility Interventions for Children in High-Poverty Neighborhoods With Subsequent Mental Disorders During Adolescence. *Journal of the American Medical Association, 311,* 937. http://doi.org/10.1001/jama.2014.607

Kikuchi, G., & Desmond, S. A. (2015). A longitudinal analysis of neighborhood crime rates using latent growth curve modeling. *Sociological Perspectives, 53,* 127–150. http://dx.doi.org/10.1525/sop.2010.53.1.127

Krivo, L. J., & Peterson, R. D. (1996). Extremely disadvantaged neighborhoods and urban crime. *Social Forces, 75,* 619–648. http://doi.org/10.1093/sf/75.2.619

Kropotkin, P. (1902). *Mutual Aid, a Factor of Evolution.* Various editions. http://doi.org/10.1038/067196a0

Lamba, S., & Mace, R. (2011). Demography and ecology drive variation in cooperation across human populations. *Proceedings of the National Academy of Sciences of the United States of America, 108,* 14426–14430. http://doi.org/10.1073/pnas.1105186108

Levine, R. V., Martinez, T. S., Brase, G., & Sorenson, K. (1994). Helping in 36 U.S. cities. *Journal of Personality and Social Psychology, 67,* 69–82.

Ludwig, J., Duncan, G. J., Gennetian, L. A., Katz, L. F., Kessler, R. C., Kling, J. R., & Sanbonmatsu, L. (2012). Neighborhood effects on the long-term well-being of low-income adults. *Science, 337,* 1505–1510.

McDade, T. W., Chyu, L., Duncan, G. J., Hoyt, L. T., Doane, L. D., & Adam, E. K. (2011). Adolescents' expectations for the future predict health behaviors in early adulthood. *Social Science and Medicine, 73,* 391–398. http://doi.org/10.1016/j.socscimed.2011.06.005

Milgram, S., Mann, L., & Harter, S. (1965). The lost-letter technique: A tool of social research. *The Public Opinion Quarterly, 29,* 437–438. http://doi.org/10.1086/267344

Miyamoto, Y., Nisbett, R. E., & Masuda, T. (2006). Culture and the physical environment holistic versus analytic perceptual affordances. *Psychological Science, 17,* 113–119. http://doi.org/10.1111/j.1467-9280.2006.01673.x

Morin, O. (2015). *How Traditions Live and Die.* Oxford: Oxford University Press.

Nettle, D. (2008). Why do some dads get more involved than others? Evidence from a large British cohort. *Evolution and Human Behavior, 29,* 416–423. http://doi.org/10.1016/j.evolhumbehav.2008.06.002

Nettle, D. (2009). An evolutionary model of low mood states. *Journal of Theoretical Biology, 257,* 100–103. http://doi.org/10.1016/j.jtbi.2008.10.033

Nettle, D. (2010a). Dying young and living fast: Variation in life history across English neighborhoods. *Behavioral Ecology, 21,* 387–395. http://doi.org/10.1093/beheco/arp202

Nettle, D. (2010b). Why are there social gradients in preventative health behavior? A perspective from behavioral ecology. *PLoS One, 5,* 6. http://doi.org/10.1371/journal.pone.0013371

Nettle, D. (2011a). Behaviour of parents and children in two contrasting urban neighbourhoods: An observational study. *Journal of Ethology, 30,* 109–116. http://doi.org/10.1007/s10164-011-0303-z

Nettle, D. (2011b). Flexibility in reproductive timing in human females: Integrating ultimate and proximate explanations. *Philosophical Transactions of the Royal Society of London. Series B, Biological Sciences, 366,* 357–365. http://doi.org/10.1098/rstb.2010.0073

Nettle, D. (2011c). Large Differences in Publicly Visible Health Behaviours across Two Neighbourhoods of the Same City. *PLoS One, 6,* e21051. http://doi.org/10.1371/journal.pone.0021051

Nettle, D. (2015). Data archive for Tyneside Neighbourhoods. *Open Science Framework*. http://doi.org/10.17605/OSF.IO/W9Z2P

Nettle, D., & Cockerill, M. (2010). Development of social variation in reproductive schedules: A study from an English urban area. *PloS One, 5*(9), e12690. http://doi.org/10.1371/journal.pone.0012690

Nettle, D., Colléony, A., & Cockerill, M. (2011). Variation in Cooperative Behaviour within a Single City. *PloS One, 6*, e26922. http://doi.org/doi:10.1371/journal.pone.0026922

Nettle, D., Coyne, R., & Colléony, A. (2012). No country for old men: Street use and social diet in urban Newcastle. *Human Nature, 23*, 375–385. http://doi.org/10.1007/s12110-012-9153-9

Nettle, D., Pepper, G. V., Jobling, R., & Schroeder, K. B. (2014). Being there: A brief visit to a neighbourhood induces the social attitudes of that neighbourhood. *PeerJ, 2*, e236. http://doi.org/10.7717/peerj.236

Nisbett, R. E. (1993). Violence and U.S. regional culture. *American Psychologist, 48*, 441–449. http://doi.org/10.1037/0003-066X.48.4.441

Nolan, J. M., Schultz, P. W., Cialdini, R. B., Goldstein, N. J., & Griskevicius, V. (2008). Normative social influence is underdetected. *Personality and Social Psychology Bulletin, 34*, 913–923. http://doi.org/10.1177/0146167208316691

Payne, G., & Payne, J. (2004). *Key Concepts in Social Research*. London: Sage.

Pepper, G. V, & Nettle, D. (2014). Perceived extrinsic mortality risk and reported effort in looking after health: Testing a behavioral ecological prediction. *Human Nature, 25*, 378–392. http://doi.org/10.1007/s12110-014-9204-5

Pickett, K. E., & Pearl, M. (2001). Multilevel analyses of neighbourhood socioeconomic context and health outcomes: A critical review. *Journal of Epidemiology and Community Health, 55*, 111–122. http://doi.org/10.1136/jech.55.2.111

Piff, P. K. (2014). Wealth and the inflated self: Class, entitlement, and narcissism. *Personality & Social Psychology Bulletin, 40*, 34–43. http://doi.org/10.1177/0146167213501699

Piff, P. K., Kraus, M. W., Côté, S., Cheng, B. H., & Keltner, D. (2010). Having less, giving more: The influence of social class on prosocial behavior. *Journal of Personality and Social Psychology, 99*, 771–784. http://doi.org/10.1037/a0020092

Pill, R., Peters, T., & Robling, M. (1995). Social class and preventive health behaviour: A British example. *Journal of Epidemiology and Community Health, 49*, 28–32. Retrieved from http://dx.doi.org/10.1136/jech.49.1.28

Rhodes, G., Jeffery, L., Watson, T. L., Clifford, C. W. G., & Nakayama, K. (2003). Fitting the mind to the world: Face adaptation and attractiveness aftereffects. *Psychological Science, 14*, 558–566. http://doi.org/10.1046/j.0956-7976.2003.psci_1465.x

Robinson, F. (2005). Regenerating the west end of Newcastle: What went wrong? *Northern Economic Review, 36*, 15–42.

Sampson, R. J. (2012). *Great American City: Chicago and the Enduring Neighborhood Effect*. Chicago: University of Chicago Press.

Sampson, R. J., Morenoff, J. D., & Gannon-Rowley, T. (2002). Assessing 'neighborhood effects': Social processes and new directions in research. *Annual Review of Sociology, 28*, 443–478. http://doi.org/10.1146/annurev.soc.28.110601.141114

Sampson, R. J., Raudenbush, S. W., & Earls, F. (1997). Neighborhoods and violent crime: A multilevel study of collective efficacy. *Science, 277*, 918–924.

Schroeder, K. B., Pepper, G. V, & Nettle, D. (2014). Local norms of cheating and the cultural evolution of crime and punishment: A study of two urban neighborhoods. *PeerJ, 2*, e450. http://doi.org/10.7717/peerj.450

Sciandra, M., Sanbonmatsu, L., Duncan, G. J., Gennetian, L. a., Katz, L. F., Kessler, R. C., Kling, J. R., Ludwig, J. (2013). Long-term effects of the Moving to Opportunity residential mobility experiment on crime and delinquency. *Journal of Experimental Criminology, 9*, 451–489. http://doi.org/10.1007/s11292-013-9189-9

Shannon, C. E. (1948). A mathematical theory of communication. *The Bell System Technical Journal, 27*, 379–423. http://doi.org/10.1145/584091.584093

Shaw, M., Tunstall, H., & Dorling, D. (2005). Increasing inequalities in risk of murder in Britain: Trends in the demographic and spatial distribution of murder, 1981-2000. *Health & Place, 11*, 45–54. http://doi.org/10.1016/j.healthplace.2004.01.003

Smaldino, P. E., Schank, J. C., & McElreath, R. (2013). Increased costs of cooperation help cooperators in the long run. *The American Naturalist, 181*, 451–463. http://doi.org/10.1086/669615

Stansfeld, S. A., & Head, J. (1998). Explaining social class differences in depression and well-being. *Social Psychiatry and Psychiatric Epidemiology, 33*, 1–9.

Stephens, D. W. (1981). The logic of risk-sensitive foraging preferences. *Animal Behaviour, 29*, 628–629. http://doi.org/10.1016/S0003-3472(81)80128-5

Talbot, E. (1997). *The Pedigree Goat in Northeast England: A History*. Newcastle: Summerhill Books.

Thaler, R., & Sunstein, C. (2008). *Nudge: Improving Decisions about Health, Wealth and Happiness*. New Yaven: Yale University Press.

Todd, S. (2014). *The People: The Rise and Fall of the Working Class*. London: John Murray.

Tooby, J., Cosmides, L., Sell, A., Lieberman, D., & Sznycer, D. (2008). Internal regulatory variables and the design of human motivation: A computational and evolutionary approach. In A. Elliott (Ed.), *Handbook of Approach and Avoidance Motivation* (pp. 251–271). Mahwah, NJ: Lawrence Erlbaum Associates.

Turnbull, C. M. (1972). *The Mountain People*. London: Jonathan Cape.

Twenge, J. M., Campbell, W. K., & Carter, N. T. (2014). Declines in trust in others and confidence in institutions among American adults and late adolescents, 1972-2012. *Psychological Science, 25*, 1914–1923. http://doi.org/10.1177/0956797614545133

Webster, M. A., Kaping, D., Mizokami, Y., & Duhamel, P. (2004). Adaptation to natural facial categories. *Nature, 428,* 557–561.

Whyte, W. H. (2009). *City: Rediscovering the Center.* Philadelphia: University of Pennsylvania Press.

Williamson, B. (1982). *Class, Culture and Community. A Biographical Study of Social Change in Mining.* London: Routledge & Kegan Paul.

Wilson, D. S., O'Brien, D. T., & Sesma, A. (2009). Human prosociality from an evolutionary perspective: Variation and correlations at a city-wide scale. *Evolution and Human Behavior, 30,* 190–200. http://doi.org/10.1016/j.evolhumbehav.2008.12.002

Winking, J., & Mizer, N. (2013). Natural-field dictator game shows no altruistic giving. *Evolution and Human Behavior, 34,* 288–293. http://doi.org/10.1016/j.evolhumbehav.2013.04.002

Young, M., & Willmott, P. (1957). *Family and Kinship in East London.* London: Routledge & Kegan Paul.

Index

This book need not end here...

At Open Book Publishers, we are changing the nature of the traditional academic book. The title you have just read will not be left on a library shelf, but will be accessed online by hundreds of readers each month across the globe. We make all our books free to read online so that students, researchers and members of the public who can't afford a printed edition can still have access to the same ideas as you.

Our digital publishing model also allows us to produce online supplementary material, including extra chapters, reviews, links and other digital resources. Find *Tyneside Neighbourhoods* on our website to access its online extras. Please check this page regularly for ongoing updates, and join the conversation by leaving your own comments:

http://www.openbookpublishers.com/isbn/9781783741885

If you enjoyed this book, and feel that research like this should be available to all readers, regardless of their income, please think about donating to us. Our company is run entirely by academics, and our publishing decisions are based on intellectual merit and public value rather than on commercial viability. We do not operate for profit and all donations, as with all other revenue we generate, will be used to finance new Open Access publications.

For further information about what we do, how to donate to OBP, additional digital material related to our titles or to order our books, please visit our website: http://www.openbookpublishers.com

OpenBook Publishers

Knowledge is for sharing

You may also be interested in:

Peace and Democratic Society
Edited by Amartya Sen

http://www.openbookpublishers.com/product/78

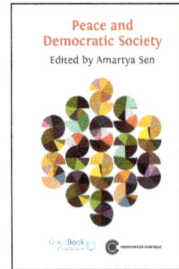

Democracy and Power. The Delhi Lectures
Noam Chomsky
Introduction by Jean Drèze

http://www.openbookpublishers.com/product/300

Economic Fables
Ariel Rubinstein

http://www.openbookpublishers.com/product/136

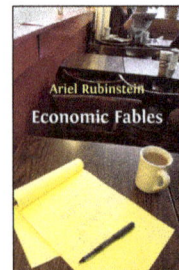

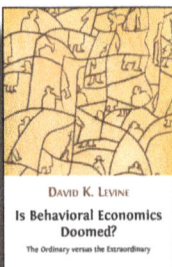

Is Behavioral Economics Doomed?
David K. Levine

http://www.openbookpublishers.com/product/77

www.ingramcontent.com/pod-product-compliance
Lightning Source LLC
Chambersburg PA
CBHW061748270326
41928CB00011B/2422

* 9 7 8 1 7 8 3 7 4 1 8 8 5 *